Gambling with God

Gambling with God

From Gambling Bartender to Born Again Christian

By

Tom Covino

Gambling with God: From Gambling Bartender to Born Again Christian by Tom Covino

ISBN: 978-0-692-81003-3

Gambling with God Publishing
210-316-1984

In the end, and at the end of your life, only one thing will matter—eternity! Because of this, there's only one question that must be answered:

Are you saved?

This is my story of how God saved me from the wrath to come, and how he can save you. Going to heaven will not be an accident. It's your choice.

Please don't gamble with God. Instead, let him save your soul.

Table of Contents

Part One: From Gambling Bartender to Born Again .... Christian.. 1

    Beginning: Breeder's Cup Day 1999........................ 3

    Chapter One 7

    Early Life (25 Years Earlier)................................... 7

    Duncan.. 9

    Chapter Two 13

    Finding Work... 13

    The Life of a Bartender... 15

    Crying Out.. 23

    God Sends a Messenger 25

    Chapter Three... 31

    Texas, Really?.. 31

    Culture Shock.. 35

    Chapter Four... 39

    The Most Important Interview of My Life 39

    Ask and You Shall Receive 43

    God's Truth vs. My Upbringing............................ 45

    Chapter Five 51

    My "Heart Attack"... 51

    Removing the Mask 53

    Higher Stakes.. 56

    Chapter Six 59

    Michael to the Rescue 59

Tom Goes to Church.................................... 61

God Sends a Preacher (I Am Saved) 65

Chapter Seven 79

Breeder's Cup: The Moment of Truth.................... 79

His Story Became Mine 80

Then What? 83

Part Two: Then What?..................................... 87

Chapter Eight 89

Finding Freedom 89

Reasons People Don't Turn to God 92

Chapter Nine 103

What God Says About Sexual Immorality.......... 103

What God Says About Adultery......................... 105

What God Says About Homosexuality............... 108

What God Says About "The Sinner's Prayer"...... 115

What God Says About Baptism.......................... 117

What Man Says About Baptism 119

Is Hell Really Worth It? Three Passages 124

What God Says About Divisions in the Church .. 128

Chapter Ten 151

Will You Gamble Your Soul on Judgment Day?..... 151

He Gambled with God No More—He Obeyed
..the Gospel.. 152

Medical Evaluation of Your Soul............................. 160

About the Author.. 165

Part One

From Gambling Bartender to Born Again Christian

Beginning: Breeder's Cup Day 1999

It was a beautiful Saturday morning in South Texas. The morning dew and slight chill were a welcome relief from the last four months of stifling heat. October was one of my favorite months. The tenth was my wedding anniversary and the twenty-eighth my birthday. There was a third day, though, that had always been marked on my mental calendar.

Breeder's Cup Day was the day when the best horses in the world raced against each other in their respective classes. I was all too familiar with this day, not as an owner or jockey, but as one who wagered his money on the outcome of all the races. Things were different now. I had a loving wife (Jennifer), two precious daughters (Gwendolyn and Aubrey), and a comfortable house in San Antonio, Texas.

I finally had a solid job as a golf professional. In fact, I owned my own teaching facility, TC's Golf Academy. I absolutely loved teaching the great game of golf. Still, though, on this Breeder's Cup Day, my heart raced in a way that it hadn't in a long time. I no longer gambled; I had given up gambling years ago.

My mind raced. *Why was I having this desire to gamble away my family's money? I have an academy to run and lessons to give. I can't go out to the horse track to make a wager. I'll just watch some of the races on television between my golf lessons. This way, I'll keep myself from placing a bet.*

"Mr. Covino, the picker on the golf cart just broke, and we can't pick the golf balls," said my assistant Randy.

Not today . . . not on a Saturday! No balls, no customers!

"I'll call the place we always call to come fix it," I said.

"We just need one little part, Mr. Covino. It's over by Retama Park. Would you like me to go pick it up?"

Did he just say Retama Park? The Retama Park Horse Track? My mind went into overdrive. My heart began to palpitate wildly. My thoughts were at war: *Should I call to see if the place is open today? No, if I call they might be closed then there is no reason to drive over past Retama Park! I have to have $200 in my pocket right now . . .* Breaking my own train of private thought, I looked Randy in the eye and said, "No Randy. I'll take care of it."

Sure enough, when I arrived at the golf supply store, it was closed. My thoughts took over: *I could turn right around and head back on the highway I had just come from, but only a half of mile more and I could turn into Retama Park Horse Track and turn my $200 into $2,000! I'm driving 70mph . . . I should slow down. The park is only a quarter of a mile ahead on the left.* I began to sweat profusely. My heart was beating out of my chest. I was out of control. I closed my eyes for a second . . .

Chapter ⚀

Early Life (25 Years Earlier)

It was the worst day of my life. I was at home when my mother confronted my father. Eight years old, I lay motionless on my bed. They fought all the time, but something inside told me the end was near. They would always remain my parents, but family life as I knew it was about to end. My pillow was not large enough or soundproof enough to drown out the yelling.

"How dare you? GET OUT!" yelled my mother.

That was the last thing I remember. From that day and for the next twenty-five years, it was as if I was wearing a mask that I could not remove. That's a long time to wear something that doesn't allow you to breathe or smile. No wonder many people were constantly asking me, "Hey Tommy, what's wrong?"

I kept things in day after day while everyone in the room, including family members, explained it away as my being shy. I bottled it up with the strongest of corks while being told, "Don't think about your father leaving" or "Pick yourself up by your bootstraps."

In the mid-1960s there was very little counseling for children of divorced parents. It just wasn't spoken about. As divorce became rampant over the next decades, it became clear that children from broken homes have a higher risk of troublesome childhood patterns: earlier sexual behavior, anger problems, and addiction issues.

I remember vividly the first time I lashed out in an unprovoked and unexpected way. I saw a beautiful little bird perched on top of the fence surrounding the tennis court at my school. For no apparent reason, yet for every hidden reason, I picked up a tennis ball and threw it as hard and accurately as I could. The mask of sadness and hate had come to life. I had killed an innocent bird; I had killed my conscience, too.

I was now a prisoner in my own jail, locked away from friends, family, and even myself. One of my biggest fears was death, yet I just killed a bird that, when soaring, was a picture of freedom and life. I trusted no one, feared no one, and chose to love no one. Although I was still alive, I felt dead inside.

I carried an oppressive chip on my shoulder vowing to play the game of life under my own rules. I played it like I played shortstop at a baseball game. When I tagged a runner out, he would never forget it.

I was bitter at every batter who dared to come to my part of the field of my life. Even my best friends felt the sting of every insult for even the slightest of mistakes. In my mind I never lost an argument and nobody could ever tell me what to do. Anger raged inside, and so did pride.

From age eight to eighteen, life was filled with a few constants. I would devote most of my time to playing sports while remaining painfully silent when anyone asked me about my parents. Sports kept my mind and body busy and away from my past, but I carried scars deep inside.

When it was time to go home from playing stick ball, basketball, wiffle ball, and football those long summer days, I would walk into the house and feel all alone. One neighbor friend of mine was a bright spot.

Duncan

Duncan was my childhood next-door neighbor. We went to school together growing up. Duncan was hilarious. His sense of humor made Duncan very popular. If Duncan was in your class, you were sure to crack up, even if you were the teacher!

When we graduated high school Duncan and his family moved away and I lost track of him. About eight years later, out of the blue, there was a knock on my door. I still lived at the home where I grew up.

Right from moment he stepped past my front door, Duncan seemed different. He wasn't laughing. In fact, he seemed about as serious as I had ever seen him. The first thing he said was, "Can I sit down on your rug, and will you join me?" I guessed Duncan was going for shock value before making me crack up, so I went along and sat on the rug. "I am a Born Again Christian" is about all I remember him saying; everything after that I completely tuned out. He got up shortly thereafter and left my house.

Less than a year later I got the terrible news that my neighbor and childhood friend Duncan had died.

My heart sank trying to figure out what would have killed someone so young. It had to be a car accident—that seemed to be how most lost their lives at such a young age. I soon learned that Duncan had committed suicide at his home.

Why would he lock himself in his parked car in his cold garage and start his car with no thoughts of driving it? What kept Duncan's mind and garage door closed while he sat in a running car? How did he arrive at the conclusion that he did not want to play this game of life anymore? Duncan seemed the happiest guy on earth. What was it that made him find death more valuable than life? The guy who made everyone laugh was crying inside. He must have been wearing a mask, too.

I didn't go to Duncan's funeral. I couldn't go to anyone's funeral. I was petrified to see anyone's lifeless body, especially that of my friend with whom I'd spent years growing up. Death scared me to death!

Where is Duncan right now? I have to know, but no one will tell me. He was only twenty-six years old. He never had the chance to get married, have kids, settle down, and experience more of life. Where is he now? Did he do enough to get to this heaven that people seem to talk about only when there is a death? Why, Duncan. Why? I thought you told me you were a "Born Again Christian." These things can't happen to a Christian, can they?

The very thought of laying a body in a casket, placing that box in the ground, and covering it with soil seemed so suffocating. *What if he wakes up?* I often woke up in the middle of my sleep. It began right after my father was told to leave. I was eight years old and having nightmares. They were not about my parents, but about my own death. I would dream once or twice a week about being struck by a car while riding my bicycle. The car would always hit me from the side. I never saw the car coming. The next thing I knew, I was lying in the casket under the ground, yet I was not dead—or if I was, I was conscious. I kept asking myself: "Now what happens? What is next? Is this all there is?"

My mother always did her best to comfort me after the nightmares: "Be a good boy, Tommy." But I still had questions. One day when I was awake, I asked my mother to explain heaven to me. She said I needed to do more good things than bad things to be able to go there. I asked the only logical question my eight-year-old brain could ask. "How do I know which I have done more of, good or bad?"

"Don't worry—God knows," said my mother.

When Duncan died, the questions swirled. *Where is Duncan now? Did Duncan do more good things than bad? Does it matter that he took his own life? Why do people have trouble speaking about suicide? Is it a sin? Will I ever see him again? Where is my father? Why isn't he here to help me through this? I wonder, did Duncan's parents got divorced, too?*

Chapter

Finding Work

I was now in my twenties, having graduated from St. John's University. My love of sports got me a baseball scholarship, but the dream of professional baseball was over. Now what? I didn't take the educational part of college seriously enough to earn a living, so I took one of the worst detours in life that a man can take. Instead of working hard, I decided to hardly work. I drifted from job to job while continuing to try to fill the same void I'd felt as long as I could remember.

I turned to gambling. It started at Roosevelt Raceway on Long Island. Yes, I won my first bet and felt alive and important. Little did I know it would lead to all-night poker games, Jai Lai in Connecticut, and betting on NFL games. My whole existence was now based on a bet.

I did grow up a bit and worked for a couple of companies selling fitness memberships—one on Long Island and the other in Manhattan. But these jobs only served as a way for me to gamble more often and with more money. Still, I had a deep determination pulling at me from the inside. I wanted to play or be known as a professional athlete. I had one last shot—golf.

My addictive behavior kicked in once again, only this time for good. Golf settled me. I had to learn to control my ball and my emotions in a game that most would call the most frustrating game in the world. As I achieved some success in breaking 80, I set my sights much higher—to become a golf professional. Although I was in my mid-late twenties, I refused to let my age deter me. As my friends snickered, I found myself challenged into overdrive.

I spent the next three years practicing seven days a week. Mom had always told me, "If you rest, you rust." My life was job during the day, sneak into Engineers Country Club by 6 p.m., and practice well into the night. I was nicknamed "Night Putter." No longer did my friends snicker, but they brought their clubs too and joined in on the fun. To my friends Billy, Pat, and most of all my brother Jimmy—you helped me find my place in sports. I gutted it out like my mom had trained me, and I became a golf pro at the ripe old age of thirty. Unfortunately, $8 an hour didn't make me feel so fortunate, so I supplemented my income in the second detour of my life, bartending.

The Life of a Bartender

It was just another night and more of the same stories. It was the same people laughing at the same things. Most of them were drinking the same drink one after the other. All of them walked in and looked for the same table they sat at the night before. Three of them found their usual places at the bar.

Barry

Barry was the first to sit at the far left side of the bar on his favorite stool with the best angle to see the television. Barry was a former tennis pro, fifty-something years old, wearing the same blue sweat pants and jacket that he had worn since the 1970s. Barry was a cordial soul, always saying a polite "hello," but keeping mostly to himself. Once again, Barry was going to get liquored up in his nice and quiet way until his reminiscing began.

"Tommy, did I tell you about the time I played against Bjorn Borg?" Last night it was Jimmy Connors. Two sets, three sets. It all changes a little bit each time, but the premise stays the same. I can see clearly what must go on in the mind of Barry the tennis pro. "I'm old and I can't play the game anymore. . . . They used to like my tennis stories. . . . I miss my wife. . . . I wish I had treated her better; maybe she would have stayed. . . . I'm so lonely; I wish I had one good friend. . . . Is life ever going to get any better for me? Sometimes I wish I would die so I wouldn't feel all the pain."

The bartender laughs when the customer laughs. He argues about sports because the customer loves it. He listens to every story as if he really cares even when the drunkard tells lie after lie, but he never, ever cries with them. Crying has the perception of weakness, and I would have no part in that. Mom always told me to wear my heart on my sleeve and to have compassion for others, but in my mind that doesn't apply when you're trying to make a buck. Serve them even when you know you shouldn't, fake it, and act like you care. Then throw them out when they don't realize a ten and a five are sitting on the bar. Well I rarely cut anyone off. No, I would schmooze with the booze until they threw their money at me. Thanks to Barry for another donation to the sad life of Tom Covino.

With the night coming to a close, everything was fine until I began the cleanup. I kept the TV on but muted it so I didn't miss the highlights that I had already watched five times. First I restocked all the beer. *Wow. People really can drink!* Next, I wiped down the bar to get rid of the sticky liquor and spilled beer. I turned on the jukebox to hear my favorite sad songs that drowned out my own serious issues. Last came the sweeping of the nasty floors. Sticky, smelly, disgusting.

So there I was in this horrible place of cigarette and alcohol stench, sweeping up filth. But then again who was I to complain about others? I had a few problems of my own, only no one knew about them—or so I thought at the time.

The only thing left to do was count the bar's money. There are no checks in the bar business, just coins, cash and "skimming off the top." A fancy phrase for stealing from the bar, I think I had even heard it called a sin. I counted two hundred and fifty dollars, including the quarters. I stuffed the money into my pocket, sat on the side where the customer sits, and had one last beer before I left.

It was 2:00 a.m., and the real working-class men would be waking in four hours—those men who had a good, steady job in the Big Apple, an adoring wife lying next to him, and a few children asleep in their beds. The perfect family. It was the exact opposite of what I was and what I had, yet it was the picture of exactly what I had always craved—something called home.

I wished I could stop thinking about my past. As a matter of fact, I wished I could stop thinking about my future, too. As I finished my beer, I was left with this indelible thought: *Today, right now, my life is a failure. I am a failure in my own eyes.* I knew how this would play out. I would fall asleep about 3:00 a.m. and wake up at

11:00 a.m. I would grab a bite and a newspaper and go straight to the horse section.

I'd begin with $250 and turn it in to five grand! These are the thoughts of every gambler who bets on the ponies. I loved it. I couldn't get enough of it. Not only did I want to pick the winner and collect the money and gloat over all the other deceived men in there with me, but the race itself was addicting. The competition was like all the baseball games I used to play. Bases were loaded and I ripped a double down the line to win the game. Better yet, it was the play up the middle at short-stop—a dive, a stab, and a backhanded toss to nip the runner as the crowd went nuts.

How the brain works I'll never know. *How does a man get past the past? How do I let go of the clutching future that hasn't even happened yet? Why am I standing next to a guy named Angelo telling him that I'm going to wager fifty of my smoky, sticky bartending dollars on a horse named "Devil's Kiss?"*

Even though I loved to gamble more than work, somehow I truly believed when I looked around the room that I just didn't belong there. That was the problem precisely. I had no idea of who I was or where I belonged. *How did I get to be thirty-two years old? I should have a good job by this age. Why can't I stay in love with a girl? Any girl? Why won't I let anyone get close to me? I'm never going to own a house. I hate my father for what he did to our family. Why do I keep dreaming about death? I think I have depression problems. Hey, I'm funny, maybe I could be an actor . . .*

And Devil's Kiss loses by a nose!

What makes it worse is that the guy next to me picked the winner and pretended to know what he was doing. At the end of the day, even with a couple of wins, I lost $175 of the $250. I got into my car, drove away, and swore I'd never go back.

Rocky

Night after night, I expected nothing new to blow into town. The bar was like a movie reel stuck on a frame. Most of the actors happened to be my regulars. Some had thick New York accents, while others caught you with their curious laughs. Rocky was a bit different from all the rest. He was a smallish man with short combed-over brown hair. He wore the type of round glasses accountants wear.

Rocky had a squeaky voice that got even higher when he talked about baseball. *Did he really just say his favorite team was the Red Sox?* As a Yankee fan, I looked to poison his gin and tonic! I noticed one other thing about Rocky. Every once in a while, he gave me a look like, "Hey, I'm trying to tell you something"—an expression of discomfort and pain deep on the inside. I think gut feelings are right on the money. So much so, that I'd often go with my instinct when it came to seeing the pains and aches of everyone else. We ended up talking for much of the night, about much more than the Red Sox or the Yankees.

At closing time Rocky didn't want our conversations to end. Without a warning sign, he started to sob right at the bar in front of me. The gin might have been the catalyst, but whatever was hurting Rocky simply needed to come out. Liquor will dull the senses until it heightens them in recollection of the truth. You see "they" had stuck Rocky's head in an oven threatening to kill him if he didn't pay his gambling debt. The horror of that encounter paled in comparison to his wife threatening to leave him if he didn't stop gambling. "They" never did turn the knob on the oven, but his wife eventually had enough, and Rocky was alone.

Ms. Fur Coat

Every bar had one—the woman who walked in and wanted all eyes to follow her. Ms. Fur Coat wore provocative clothing and desperately wanted to be noticed and left alone at the same time. She probably ordered a martini and smoked a long cigarette. She was not in the right place from my point of view, but from hers, she was right where she needed to be for the night. She needed eyes on her to feel attractive and powerful—more importantly, to feel needed.

"Small talk?"

"Yes!"

"Can I buy you a drink?"

"Sure!"

But that's where it ended. She was hopelessly in love with her husband who had just left her for another. She was starving for affection and intimacy; she was broken-hearted inside. She smiled in a way detectable to any bartender– the upside-down frown. I continued to serve her drink after drink, yet I ignored her minute after minute. The night was getting late, two or three in the morning by now. It had begun snowing much earlier, and the temperature had dropped quickly. Getting home would be an ice-filled thrill ride. It was another cold, wet, icy New York winter.

The thoughts assailed me: *What am I doing here and why am I a bartender? "Last Call for Alcohol!"*

People begin to trickle out of the bar. I said my goodbyes to Rocky and Barry. I went downstairs to restock the beer and took my time. I had completely forgotten about Ms. Fur Coat at the bar. Suddenly, I heard a noise and realized she was stumbling around in the ladies' bathroom. Out she came, and I quickly went to her and escorted her to the door. "Let me get the door for you; it's way past closing time. Be careful going home. See you soon." (*I hope not.)* All was right once again, or so I thought. As I prepared to exit the bar and make my way home, she walked right back in the same way she left—drunk and stumbling.

In her slurred Long Island accent she mumbled, "There's aysh (ice) on your wingshiad (windshield); lemme have that aysh skrapa (ice scraper) and I'll clean it for ya."

I told her, "Don't worry about it."

"No, I said I'll clean it for ya—gimme it!"

"Let go, lady!"

I had an all-out ice-scraper-yanking battle with Ms. Fur Coat and I thought I was going to lose. One last yank and I finally survived. Quickly I flew inside the bar and locked myself in. Case closed. Case not closed. She walked toward my car. My 1980 dirt colored Honda hatchback sat like prey. Suddenly, for one brief moment, it was like everything stopped. Her head flipped over her heels, and she was on the slick ground in an instant. She slowly pulled herself to her feet and stumbled away. I should have just given her the ice scraper.

Barry, Rocky, and Ms. Fur Coat were my life for those years as a bartender in New York. Day by day, night by night, I listened to their conversations, identified with their hopelessness, and wondered when life would change.

Crying Out

Most of us, myself included, fail to realize the subtle life-changing events that happen quietly during our days. My only life-altering event thus far had been the day when our family was broken up. The rest of the time I was living like a feather in the breeze, moved along wherever the winds would blow. Little did I know, that was all about to change.

I had been at the pub serving alcohol as usual. Tuesday nights were usually slow. I didn't particularly mind. I'd make a few bucks and leave before midnight. Still, the winter chill and dark early skies brought me down. I was tired of the same routine. I didn't want to be there anymore, but I needed the money for my gambling habit. I was miserable. Even though I was in a dating relationship, it was only a matter of time before we would go our separate ways. I put off breaking up so that I could pretend I was happy.

After making a mere $100 in tips and $200 in video bowling gambling winnings, I left for home. I didn't like myself at all. I worked for $100, gambled for $200. I was sick to my stomach for taking a friend's money and afraid this was going to be my life forever.

I cannot explain it any better than this. Instead of going upstairs to my apartment that night when I arrived home, I went around the back of the house.

Standing outside and looking up at the stars, anger and fury rose inside of me. With my right hand clenched and eyes fixed upward, I yelled loudly enough for all my neighbors to hear me, "IF YOU ARE REAL, DO SOMETHING IN MY LIFE! IS THIS WHAT YOU CREATED ME FOR—TO SWEEP UP AFTER DRUNK PEOPLE?"

I'm not sure what I expected, but there was no response. Just the quiet. Seemingly, I had spoken only to the stars and moon. I don't know why I did that. I guess I was trying to express to God how frustrated I was with this so-called life. I needed to tell him he hadn't helped me along one bit. *Whom was I kidding?* I didn't know God, and it seemed to me He surely didn't care about me. I figured I had done more bad things than good.

I went up to my apartment as if nothing had happened. I lay awake, my mind racing. *This is my life; I have no meaning and I have no purpose.* I thought about Duncan. He had to have been in the same position before he decided to take his own life. Did I contemplate that too? You bet I did. Every losing gambler probably does. Losing money is one thing, but losing at life is another. I didn't want this kind of life anymore.

God Sends a Messenger

The daily ups and downs of life resumed for me. I was totally unaware that my life was in the early stages of a drastic change. Not long after my shout to the stars, I was invited to a party in New York City. Having already experienced that hustle and bustle as a bartender, I knew all too well that the thrill would be temporary. I had seen it countless times before. Yet this night had something different in store for me. This was a party for a buddy of mine. I was there to do what everyone else was doing: drink, talk, and be thankful not to be home alone. Ten years removed from high school, I ran into an old wrestling teammate, Charlie. We were both at the same party in one of the biggest cities in the world. Coincidence?

As Charlie and I got caught up on life, he told me he was very much into playing golf. We had a lot to talk about because I had been working as a beginner golf pro during the day while bartending at night. Charlie, however, was playing golf because he was a very successful lawyer with clients and free time. As usual, I started to compare my life with others and see that the ledger was positive on his side and negative on mine. I felt the cards of life had been dealt unfairly. For some odd reason, it didn't bother me the way it usually did. Something was different about Charlie. He didn't talk and act like the typical lawyer with an attitude. He was normal Charlie—sincere, funny, and about to offer the kindest of gestures.

"TC, would you like to come on our trip to Scotland to play golf at St. Andrews?"

"I'm sorry, but I don't have the money to travel," I replied.

Without any hesitation at all, he made an offer I could not refuse. It was the way that he did it I will always remember. Not with any broadcast or words to make me feel guilty, he said, "I'll take care of it all. If I was in the same position, you'd do it for me."

The truth is, no I wouldn't have. I knew me. I accepted his generous offer and was about to take the first good gamble of my life.

Finally! The day was here. I met the two other guys at the airport. Their names were Dave and Collier. They were both very successful and cordial. Collier was a member of the famed Winged Foot Country Club. Dave was a member of the San Francisco Club and had played Augusta National. I felt instantly out of my league, but then again that was because I saw them living out my dream. Regardless, I was so excited to play the "Old Course" and experience the wind, large bunkers, and the men who would carry my bag and speak with the dialect of their homeland. It was a dream come true.

Charlie warned me before I teed off on #1 that I shouldn't take a practice swing and that I should wait for the starter to introduce me. "Next on the tee, Tom … (*Oh please don't say Corvito, Corvino, Covina, or my all-time favorite Constapino*) Covino." Yes! He got it right! I smoked it down the middle, 7-iron to the green, and sank the putt for birdie.

I was a good person again because I played good golf. That was how my mind worked. But that thought didn't last long. I made some typical mistakes, got caught up in the view of each army-tank-sized bunker, listened to the caddy exchanges to see if I could understand one word, and noticed that the wind had changed the part in my hair from the left to the right. I birdied the first and the last to finish with a 79. All was good for now, but it wouldn't last. It never did.

A few hours later, Charlie and I were driving on the roads of Scotland when he began to cross-examine me like a good lawyer. The front seat of that itty-bitty car felt like a witness stand.

"How is the family?" he asked.

No time to cave in now. "You know, same as usual, Charlie." What a fake I was. I knew, though, that if I let any of it out, the whole thing would come flowing out.

He had just asked me about my family in a way that I never sensed before. He wasn't looking for the obligatory response just to pass time; he truly wanted to know. *I don't think I can tell him. I can't cry in front of anybody, let alone a guy who thinks I have my act together.* I slowly explained that my relationship with my father was nonexistent. The typical response for most people was, "I'm sorry to hear that."

But Charlie said, "I try not to judge those situations because somebody else already has that job."

I asked, "Who?"

Without hesitation, he answered, "Jesus Christ."

There may have been a long uncomfortable silence in the car, but in my heart a healing symphony had begun to play. Time slowed down on that road trip through Scotland. I could sense something totally unique was about to happen in my life. I felt a rare calm as the name of Jesus Christ rested in my heart and mind.

Charlie and I became good friends. We played golf, grabbed a bite to eat here and there, and had significant conversations. One day he gave me the best advice when it came to relationships between men and women. I had told him I had been dating a girl for five years. I explained that I didn't know where the relationship was going.

He asked, "Do you love her?"

I said, "I don't know!"

He answered, "When you don't know, you know."

There it was—the truth coming to the surface, the truth I'd suppressed for quite some time. I ended my relationship with the young lady who only gave me her best. Strangely enough, my best was letting her go.

Chapter ⚁

Texas, Really?

With the trip from Scotland in my rearview mirror and things settling back into the old routine, I continued my life of assistant golf professional by day and bartender by night. At least I worked at a local country club that had a great group of members. The pro, Doug, made the bucks, and he made the rules. He told me I would be working twenty-eight days a month.

My job entailed everything imaginable in any cleaning business not having to do with teaching or playing golf: taking orders, folding the shirts, dusting the racks, vacuuming the rug. Does Doug know how I used to live? I shared bunk beds with my younger brother in such a small room that Harry Houdini could not escape. The clothes on our bedroom floor were from two seasons ago; I was a domestic slob and Doug had me in charge of cleaning! Nevertheless, I had come to take pride in my work. I did it all for an earth-shattering salary of $10,000 per year.

"By the way, Tom, when you lock up at night, go down to the barn and re-grip as many of the member's clubs as you'd like. We'll pay you a dollar each."

As time marched slowly by and the days seemed endless and still, I was awakened one day to the sound of the phone ringing at the crack of dawn. Doug told me I needed to be ready right away to play nine holes with Boomer Esiason, quarterback of the New York Jets. I thought to myself, *Doug, thanks to you I no longer know how to play golf. I could re-grip his clubs or fold his clothes, but I cannot come out of my cage and play golf!*

I lied. "Sounds great, Doug! Can't wait!"

All I could think about was how desperately I wanted to get the ball in the air. Somehow, I birdied three of the nine holes and helped Boomer win $350, of which I got none. He invited me for drinks with the rest of the bigwigs until my task master broke up the party and sent me back to my shirt-folding dungeon.

Days later, after vacuuming and dusting racks, I'd had enough. I accosted Doug and demanded to know how I was ever going to succeed financially in the golf business. He immediately said, "Move to Texas!"

Texas? Really? Who in the world would ever want to live in Texas?

While in the pro shop one day not long after that, I received a call from Charlie. "Tommy, I'm getting married to Emma. We're moving to London. I'm going to have a going-away party in a few weeks, and I want you to join us."

Of course my first thoughts were selfish. My good friend who took me to Scotland, talked to me about my family in an open and honest way, and brought up Jesus Christ had found the perfect girl and was going to abandon me!

"That is awesome! Of course, I'll be there."

As I had a few days to digest the news, I reflected on how fortunate I had been to reconnect with Charlie at that party in Manhattan. Meeting him again was one of the best things that had happened in a long time in my life. A couple more days passed, and I got another phone call from him. He told me he just met a girl in the city that he would like me to meet at his going-away party. He had told her about me and she was looking forward to meeting me. I thought there was no way a complete stranger would show up to his party.

The night of Charlie's party I had dismissed all thoughts of this mystery girl showing up. However, she was there. That had to be her. After we met I don't think I spoke to anybody else at party the rest of the night. I was drawn to this girl, only I couldn't quite figure out why yet. She was not from New York, of that I could be sure. She was dressed differently from what I was used to seeing around the city. She seemed wholesome and simple. Her name was Sheila. She traveled the world, spoke French, was a concierge at a cool hotel in the city, and had an apartment near Central Park. But New York was not her home. Texas was.

Sheila and I dated for the next six months. I found out all about her life in San Antonio, and she learned about my life in New York. I wanted to put my best foot forward, and I wanted to hide my ugly side. Revealing my true self would be a gamble in itself. I wasn't ready to show my cards just yet.

I did find it easier than normal to open up about some of my problems and failures of the past. Sheila was an open book, something I was not accustomed to. Growing up, Mom always would tell us about some problems in the family, but that we shouldn't speak about them. Of course, I, the thinker who questioned everything, questioned this too. Back in those days, when my heart was shattered at the age of eight, I kept everything inside concerning my parents' divorce. You just didn't talk about things like that.

As Sheila opened up about her life in an effortless way, I began to take a couple of steps. Mine looked like the seventh-grade boy at his first dance trying to find rhythm: stand in one place and move my arms a little and believe that I was dancing. I moved my mouth a little and a few words came out, but I wasn't too sure that I had said anything of great value. At least it was a start.

After we had been dating for several months, Sheila received a devastating phone call in the middle of the night. The person in her life that filled her up the most was her brother. He was critically ill, and Sheila needed to move back to San Antonio to take care of him. What's strange is the fact that I knew I occupied second place in her heart to her brother, and yet I was okay with that. Sheila was constantly on the phone with her mom arranging the move back home. I stayed out of the way letting her do what was needed.

I assumed Sheila was going to go home to take care of her brother for a few months and then come back to New York. But she told me that she was permanently moving back to Texas. After a long pause, she asked, "Would you move down with me?"

After no pause at all, I answered, "Yes! Of course, I will."

Culture Shock

I hadn't thought it through. *I have no savings. I would have no job. At least I would get a new accent. From "you guys" to "y'all," sneakers to "tennies" (tennis shoes), Italian food to Mexican, baseball cap to cowboy hat, the Hustle to the Two Step. I am moving to Texas, home of the Longhorns and the San Antonio Spurs. Party down at the River Walk and—100 degree days of sweltering heat.*

I remember the day of my departure, October 17, 1994. I will never forget it. My only brother Jimmy (nicknamed Rat) took me to La Guardia Airport. I packed all I had to my name—a suitcase of clothes and my golf clubs. I remember saying goodbye to Jimmy and knowing that I wouldn't be back except to visit. I think he knew it, too. Even though my brother and I fought a lot when we were younger, there was an unspoken bond between us. We both knew that the other one was deeply wounded by the separation of our parents. We were athletes, brothers, and most importantly, survivors together. I could sense that he knew that this was the best thing for me. I didn't belong in New York anymore. Even my grandmother had told me just months before that she thought New York wasn't the best fit for me.

"Take care Jimmy C.," I said.

"See ya, Bro."

I went through the security line and never looked back.

When I landed in the Lone Star State, Sheila picked me up, and we went driving around the city. She took me to lunch. Now that's a burger! Texas is proud of their barbecue and their burgers, too. Having finished a quick driving tour of the city, it was time to find out where we were going to pitch our tent. I noticed right away that the drive was becoming long and the buildings and people were becoming few. Like a pioneer heading West, I began looking for tumble-weeds and dust storms.

As I began to feel like an Italian without a country, we finally arrived what would be called home. It was a pleasant place only five minutes from a lake. The house was about 2,500 square feet, more than double the size I grew up in. We were greeted by all of Sheila's family. They all seemed like wonderful people. Right away the show "Dallas" came to my mind and a little bit of "Green Acres" too. But all in all, it was a welcoming start.

That evening I took stark note of my surround-ings—I was in the middle of nowhere with only a Sac-N-Pac grocery nearby. I took a drive, stopped at the nearest pay phone and called my brother. I told him I was at Sac-N-Pac. I told him that there was one gas station and that Andy Griffith and Barney Fife were working there. I also told him there was no way that I could live here. I was stuck in the country.

To Sheila I presented a different story: "Every-thing's great and I love it here."

We lived together in the house, a few miles from a lake and all I could think of was going back home. I hadn't even told her that I had a grand total of $3,500 dollars to my name with no job and no prospects. How in the world would I be able to start over? I thought a lot about what my mother taught me through sports. She was the one who threw the football and baseball with us. She imprinted on my mind that if the fastest way to get the ball was through the tree, then run through it. She told me that I was a late bloomer, but that I was a fighter. "Don't quit. Keep going. You can do anything that you want." I leaned on those principles as a young athlete, and again as an adult searching for a job.

When no one offered me a job right away, I called the PGA employment hotline. There were two opportunities: one at a club in Houston and the other was at a driving range in San Antonio that was not even open yet. *Had I come all this way only for another dead end?*

Chapter ⚃

The Most Important Interview of My Life

I convinced first myself and then Sheila that this was going to be the opportunity of a lifetime. I gave a call to the not-yet-open, still-under-construction golf range and was told they were looking for an assistant to the head pro. I said all the right things and got invited for an interview.

Driving to the interview, I got lost in a series of highway loops like I had never seen before. There was Loop 410, I-10, Hwy 281, and my favorite, Loop 1604. Where was Times Square or the Long Island Expressway? Navigating New York was a breeze compared to this! I heard a siren and was pulled over for driving a bit faster than I should have been. *Didn't the officer know that I was on my way to the interview of my life? Didn't he realize that I was still lost?* Seeing my New York driver's license, he quipped, "You Yankees think you can drive as fast as you want down here!"

Now if I had played shortstop with the Yankees or was as fortunate as George Costanza to work for the front office, then I might have appreciated being called a Yankee, but I didn't. Even though I was raised to respect authority, I couldn't resist the urge to put him in his place. I snapped back some sarcastic remark, knowing it was a gamble. With a look of surprise, the officer took my license and went back to his car. When he didn't immediately reach for the handcuffs, I was relieved to have got away with my counter punch. He returned and handed me back my New York driver's license and told me to slow down and have a nice day. *No ticket! Maybe Texas won't be so bad after all. This was going to be my day!*

I finally found my destination: 16900 Blanco Road. I got out of my rental car, walked toward the building, and met Dan Monroe, the first person I knew in Texas other than Sheila's family. Right away I knew I would hit it off well with Dan.

He asked me if I had played many "turrnaments." Without correcting his strange pronunciation, I told him that yes, I had played in some local pro "torenaments" over the years.

He joked like the boys back home. "Torenaments! What's a torenament?"

With a mild jab back, I said, "Do they play on the PGA Turr or Tour?" *His next retort would probably decide my fate. Had I blown it already? Or was this the exact thing I needed to be true to who I really am?*

He said, "You must be from Joysie, where you watch Doity Boids on the Coib eating Woims."

I loved this guy! Back in New York all the names end in the letter Y. There's Ricky, Bobby, Tommy, Jimmy, Freddie, Vinny, and Joey. As much as I wanted to, I couldn't bring myself to call him Danny. Not yet, anyway. Dan was the owner of the facility. In my mind, I had just hit the jackpot.

Dan's wife Carolyn showed me around the facility. The name was going to be Panther Springs Golf. It had grass-hitting bays, a gigantic putting green, a retail pro shop, and all the makings of a place I knew I wanted to work. Carolyn then threw what we would call in baseball a floater. "Tom, you don't have to work on Sundays if you worship, and you can wear shorts when you give lessons."

Me give lessons? Shorts in the golf business? Worship what?

Carolyn interrupted my thoughts. "I would like you to meet our head professional, Michael Richards."

After we shook hands, we walked over to the hitting area just outside the pro shop. He wanted me to hit a few golf shots.

"Sure, Mr. Richards. Which club?"

"How about a 7-iron?" he said.

Like Roy McAvoy in *Tin Cup* (without the looks of Kevin Costner), I love my 7-iron. I don't miss with my 7-iron. Michael gave me the cherry on top when he asked if I could hit him a draw. *Am I in Kansas? Is this a funny joke from the boys back home? My interview was going to be based on my ability to hit my favorite shot with my favorite club of all time?*

"Sure, Mr. Richards."

A perfect high drawing 7-iron curved left into the red flag.

"How about a fade, Tom?"

It was more of a straight shot, but it was well struck.

I'm thinking next he'd ask, "Let's try driver," or "Sink some putts."

I was not prepared for his next question: "Tom, are you saved?"

I had made great grades in elementary school, good grades in middle school, okay grades in high school, and barely earned a college diploma. But all those years in school had not prepared me for this question that I didn't even understand. I knew, at least, he was talking about something to do with religion. I had to respond somehow.

"Excuse me, saved from what?" I asked.

"Are you going to heaven?" he asked me.

I said, "I'm Roman Catholic—but not practicing."

I don't remember the rest of the interview except
for Mr. Richards telling me to expect a call in a few
days. In those few days of waiting for the call, the only
thing on my mind was his question: "Are you saved?"

Ask and You Shall Receive

I got the call from Mr. Richards a few days later
telling me the job was mine. He asked me to come in
to talk about my schedule and responsibilities. I was
relieved to know that I was going to have a job, but I
felt an altogether different emotion gnawing inside.

When I saw Mr. Richards I quickly thanked him
for the job. Just as quickly, my question came gushing
out. "Can you tell me what you meant by asking me if
I'm saved?"

He must've anticipated that I might ask, because
he was ready to answer the question with a gift. He
gave me a Bible and told me to start reading in the
book of Genesis and the book of Matthew. He showed
me how and where to find them. Before long I went
from reading the racing form at the horse tracks to
reading the Bible.

I immersed myself in this book. I had no idea
what I had hoped to gain from reading the Bible; I only
knew that the more I read the more I wanted to read.

"In the beginning, God created the heavens and the earth" (Genesis 1:1) is something I always believed, but when I read it for myself, it meant something to me. It was personal, as if someone was reading to me. That someone was Almighty God.

I had always heard about Adam and Eve, but it wasn't until I read about them that I believed in them as real people that God had really created. As I read about the Garden of Eden and what happened to them with the first sins they committed, I began to compare myself to them. I also took notice of how they used excuses for their actions. I couldn't help but think that the reasons for so many of my poor decisions in life were based on my parents' divorce. Even though I hurt so badly inside and felt so betrayed by my father, I started to realize that I was still accountable for my choices. No matter the circumstances, every person is accountable for the choices he makes, even if those choices are influenced by hardships. Eve sinned, involved her husband Adam, and he sinned too. God found them both equally guilty for their choices. Now I know why women have labor pains. I also know why men have to work by the sweat of their brow. It is all because of sin.

The most important thing I realized when reading the beginning of the book of Genesis is that everyone must physically die. One of sin's consequences is that all men will die. No wonder I was always afraid to go to funerals. Not only were they so final, but it's true, you die and then your fate is really in the hands of the God that made everything that you look at each and every day. He made the stars that wow us. He put the moon where we could see it from time to time. God is the Creator of all the blue sky in the world. When it rains, it's because He has decided that the ground needs water. It's not Mother Nature who sets the earth and all its beauty in motion; it's God the Father who is in control over the weather in Texas and New York, Italy and Scotland.

I read and read and read some more. I didn't understand everything I was reading but it didn't matter. As I began to read the book of Matthew, I came to the conclusion that this book contained the most important thing for every man to believe, the truth.

God's Truth vs. My Upbringing

I was raised as a Roman Catholic. Actually, I was told I was born as a Roman Catholic. This wasn't a bad thing. I did not have religion pushed on me at all. I simply referred to myself and the rest of my family as Catholic. One thing I liked was that my only require-ment was attending a mass two times a year—once for Easter and then again for Christmas. I also remember going to catechism as a young teen where I would learn more about the Catholic faith. One thing that still stands out is that the teachers told me to not read the Bible; the pope would do that for us. Apparently, he alone could understand it. I was not to attempt to interpret any of the passages. This was not a problem for me at the time; I was more than happy to have no responsibility.

The biggest thing that I remember from those days was the few times I went to confession. I would go into a dark booth with a sliding window and confess my sins to a priest. I would be speaking of my wrong-doings to a man I was supposed to call "Father." I would have to start off saying, "Bless me, Father, for I have sinned." The priest's response was usually, "Say five Hail Marys." It never made sense to me, but it was part of our routine.

My mother always taught us to be respectful. She said that how we treated people mattered. I was cordial and respectful when it came to the authority of the church, but was not satisfied with the reasoning for some of the things they said to me. Mom was my hero. She did it all. She supplied all things necessary for three children to survive. She did so much more, though. She played ball with me. She took long night-time walks with us, told us to follow our dreams. She cooked, cleaned, worked, and nurtured. She was there for me when my heart was broken. She reminded me often it was better to wear my heart on my sleeve and feel pain because I would also feel great joy. However, we did not talk about God or Jesus Christ in a direct way. The only thing I knew about religion was that I was Catholic.

As I began to read the Scriptures out of the Bible that Michael gave me, I noticed word for word what Jesus was saying to the religious groups and common folks of that day. He said, "But when you pray, go into your room and shut the door and pray to your Father who is in secret. And your Father who sees in secret will reward you" (Matthew 6:6). Another time in the book of Luke a religious leader called a Pharisee, prayed and said, "God, I thank you that I am not like other men, extortioners, unjust, adulterers, or even like this tax collector. I fast twice a week; I give tithes of all that I get." The story continues, "But the tax collector, standing far off, would not even lift up his eyes to heaven, but beat his breast, saying, 'God, be merciful to me, a sinner!'" (Luke 18:11-13).

I was floored. This man spoke and confessed his sins directly to God! He did not confess to a priest. Next Jesus said, "I tell you, this man went down to his house justified, rather than the other. For everyone who exalts himself will be humbled, but the one who humbles himself will be exalted" (Luke 18:14). What Jesus was teaching me was that not only could I speak to God without anyone else present, but that I didn't need to confess to a priest either. I could confess my sin to God, and I didn't need to offer any special prayers to receive His forgiveness.

As I continued to read, another passage got my quick attention. "Not everyone who says to me, 'Lord, Lord,' will enter the kingdom of heaven" (Matthew 7:21). *What? Now I am very confused! How could what my mother said not be true? Doing more good things than bad may not be enough to get in to heaven. I have never even called Jesus, Lord. Now I read that even if I did, it might not be enough. How does this work?* I knew I had to keep reading.

Next, I read a story about a man named Zacchaeus. He was a rich tax collector. His heart yearned to see Jesus. He was a short man in size, so much that he could not see over the crowd. He climbed up a sycamore tree just to get a glimpse of the Son of God. Jesus noticed him because of his desire to follow him. He said to Zacchaeus, "Today salvation has come to this house, since he also is a son of Abraham. For the Son of Man came to seek and to save the lost" (Luke 19:9-10).

There was that word that Mr. Richards used, save. Are you saved? I had also been asked something similar years ago by my childhood friend Duncan and by Charlie when we were in Scotland. I understood that the opposite of saved was lost. If I am not saved, then

I am lost. I started to imagine what that really meant. I now knew that losing spiritually means not going to heaven. *Where did I stand? I am Catholic, but does that mean I am saved?*

I kept reading and reading. As I began to question the rituals and doctrine of my youth, it spurred me to read more and dig deeper into the Scriptures. Reading the Bible opened my eyes and heart to Jesus and a religion I'd never known. Rather than the rituals of my upbringing, I was reading about a Savior and healer who offered compassion and mercy. I read about a God who desired that no one be lost, but that all should be saved.

God says in Scripture, "So faith comes from hearing, and hearing through the word of Christ" (Romans 10:17). As I spent time in the Word of God, my faith was beginning to take shape. God's Word lay out the facts of the account. These facts were corroborated by the testimony of the witnesses. Like anything else in my life, I had to be convinced by facts that could be proven. I read the book as if they were the facts of a case. I believed the testimony. When that happened, I began believing every word. I read some things that started to convict me about my life.

I had a bitter and unforgiving heart toward my dad because of the divorce that the family went through. I had a gambling problem. I lied to hide my true self. All of these problems or habits of mine Jesus addressed in the Scriptures. One passage really got my attention. "But if you do not forgive others their trespasses, neither will your Father forgive your trespasses" (Matthew 6:15). God had my attention! I believed. I think I had wanted to believe my entire life.

My daily life started to change, but I couldn't really explain it. I had only been living in San Antonio for six months, yet I felt like this was home. Every day felt like a peeling away of sorts. The layers of doubt, anger, frustration, and depression were being removed one by one. I knew it was because I was reading the Bible.

Chapter ⚄

My "Heart Attack"

Growing up, I was always more comfortable when I was alone. I had a lot of practice! I kept my emotions hidden by my Halloween mask, only to reveal them when I played a sport or game of some kind. Golf was the perfect game because of the beautiful surroundings and the challenge of trying to perfect the imperfectible. Playing alone on the golf course was not new to me. As far as I knew, this day would be like any other eighteen-hole round of golf. It wouldn't be until the eleventh tee that I would find out otherwise.

I didn't keep score that day, at least not consciously or on the scorecard. I began this round at La Cantera simply to have some alone time. I didn't want the starter to put me with another group. I wanted to play golf, drive the cart, look at my surroundings, think and reflect, and not have to respond to anyone else's shots or conversations. La Cantera, the future home of the Texas Open, was a hilly scenic course with views of the Texas Hill Country and San Antonio's famous Six Flags Fiesta Texas amusement park.

After playing the first ten holes I came to the eleventh tee box. I suddenly dropped to my knees. I know that if there had been a group behind me they would have rushed to my aid. If they had seen my head drop to the ground, they would have been convinced I was having a heart attack. Though my physical heart was perfectly healthy, I was having an attack of my spiritual heart, and it couldn't wait. In that moment, I knew I needed help, so I asked for it.

"God, please help me. I don't know what to do. I don't know how to live. I only know that I am a lost sinner." I didn't know what to do because my pride wouldn't allow me to ask anyone, at least not very often. I never used the word sinner as part of my vocabulary until now. *So why was I speaking into the wind to a God I'd never known?*

"For the word of God is living and active, sharper than any two-edged sword, piercing to the division of soul and of spirit, of joints and of marrow, and discerning the thoughts and intentions of the heart. And no creature is hidden from his sight, but all are naked and exposed to the eyes of him to whom we must give account" (Hebrews 4:12-13). The Bible, the Word of God that I had been reading for weeks was slicing me open with every word on the page, piercing my heart.

Scripture had been telling me about who I was and, more importantly, who He is. I had started to understand why I did the things I did. *Right* and *wrong* are terms the world uses, but *righteous* and *sinner* are the terms that God uses. I was starting to understand from Jesus Christ Himself that there is a spiritual war going on that all people are part of. Most in the world have no idea they are involved. I feel like I won my first battle when I dropped to my knees on that eleventh tee box.

What battle? Repentance. I was turning from a life with no meaning except pleasing myself, and turning in the direction of Almighty God. I can't explain how or why God got my attention that day. More than making the turn to play the back nine, I'd made a turn toward Jesus in my heart and life. I finished my round, not caring how I played, only thinking that I was glad to have bowed my heart on the very ground God had created.

Removing the Mask

The next morning, I headed to work feeling like a man just set free from prison. I kept thinking about my dad. Usually when I thought about my dad, it stirred up anger and venom. But not today. Something was different. I didn't feel the burden of holding a grudge; I realized it was the grudge that had been holding onto me. As the grudge had disappeared, so had the mask I'd worn since the day my father left. I could breathe and think in a way I never had before. The only thing that came to my mind was God. He must have something to do with this.

As a seventeen-year-old, I had written a poem while overlooking the Long Island Sound. I had been bottling up feelings for nine years, and one day all the emotion came flooding out in a poem. As an adult, I carried the poem in my mind, describing my feelings for so long as I wore the mask:

> I cried when they divorced,
> Denied a guiding course,
> A man before my time,
> I taste of bitter wine,
> I pretend it not to bother,
> Growing up without a father,
> I search for the solution,
> To my private execution,
> Wounded I must strive
> To dream of family life,
> So if by chance I wed,
> I'll remember what I've said,
> To know the other side,
> When at last I have a child,
> And throughout their tender years

I'll help them conquer doubt and fears,
With my memory as my guide
I'll remember how I cried.

Now, my tears of pain had been removed and replaced with tears of freedom. In His way and time, God was teaching me about forgiveness. I had never felt so free from anything in my life.

My anger, rage, wrath, bitterness, and frustration toward my father vanished. I couldn't explain it at the time, but I was overcome with a desire to forgive my dad and apologize for staying away so long. And just like that, I decided to call him. "Dad, will you forgive me for staying away for so long? I am so sorry."

He was speechless for a few seconds and then said for the first time that I remember, "Tommy, I love you."

I saw Michael at the range soon after I'd called my dad. I know Michael had no idea I was thinking about my dad, but he knew something was going on. He saw my face and said, "Something has changed with you."

I told him I was thinking about God every day. "I can't get Him off my mind, and I don't want to." I couldn't explain exactly what happened on that eleventh tee except for the fact that I had a "letting go" of sorts. I was doing what God says that every man must do to be saved. I was drawing near to God and He was drawing near to me (James 4:8).

God says, "Whoever exalts himself will be humbled, and whoever humbles himself will be exalted" (Matthew 23:12). I wanted to follow God, but I didn't know what God meant about being exalted. I scarcely could comprehend what it meant to humble oneself until I looked it up. It means to take a position of low regard and to look out for the interests of others. It is the opposite of proud and arrogant. Getting down on my knees that day at La Cantera may have been the first time in my life that I had achieved that state of humbleness.

Higher Stakes

I was reading God's Word, absorbing it, and learning to live the way God intended me to live. That was the pattern for the next few months. I didn't know if I was saved, but as I read, I believed. And as I believed, I tried to follow. I discovered that faith is more than an arbitrary feeling inside the physical heart. I know that sounds brash and almost insincere but God told me, through His Word (the Bible) a second time that "faith comes from hearing, and hearing through the word of Christ" (Romans 10:17), and then He says "And without faith it is impossible to please Him" (Hebrews 11:6).

No wonder I didn't have faith growing up. I was told not to read Scriptures; only the pope and the priests were to read the Word of God because I wouldn't be able to understand it. At first, it made me angry, but later I would become concerned because all my family and friends back home were probably told the same thing.

Jesus tells us, "I am the way, and the truth, and the life. No one comes to the Father except through me" (John 14:6). Jesus also said to the religious Jews of the day who didn't believe He was the Messiah, "You are of your father the devil, and your will is to do your father's desires" (John 8:44). It was at this point that I was starting to really understand the spiritual war that goes on. God is 100% truth; the devil is 100% lies. There are no such things as "little white lies." Either the thing is true or false.

One of the lies I believed was that living with my girlfriend before getting married was okay because we would find out if we were compatible. If we were emotionally and sexually compatible, then that would be a good indicator of whether the marriage would work. That is a lie! I never wanted to get married because of the failed marriage of my parents. I didn't want to say to my children one day, "We are getting divorced" and have them experience that same devastating pain that I had. I didn't want them to experience the "can't take off the mask" feeling. God says that sex before marriage is a sin. *But what about all the movies and television shows? What about all the high school and college days of experimentation? Is being a virgin until marriage God's will for both men and women?* These questions were being replayed in my mind day after day until I took another gamble.

"Sheila, I need to move out since we're not married." I almost wish she had been angry. Instead, she was wounded.

"Don't you love me anymore? Aren't you attracted to me?"

"Yes, but God doesn't want me to live like this anymore. To Him it is sin."

Moving out of Sheila's place was one of many lifestyle changes I believe God wanted me to make at the time. I wasn't perfect, but I felt God changing me and turning my life toward Him.

Chapter ⚅

Michael to the Rescue

Although Sheila and I did not marry, there will always be two profound things I will take to my grave with me about our time together. Both of them would be in the form of questions posed by Sheila. She asked, "Why can't we get married?" I answered that I had found God and wanted to follow that path. She once had religion but wasn't interested in it at that point in her life. The other question she asked was, "If this is from God, then what is in it for me?"

I answered, "If you hadn't met Charlie and if you hadn't decided to go to his party and if I hadn't met you then, I would not have found God. Sheila, you brought me to where God wanted me to be. I hope that can be enough for you." Many years have passed, yet I believe with all my heart that she has taken some comfort that she was a part of God's plan to help save me.

With no place to live, I needed to start looking for an apartment of my own. I didn't have to look long because Michael came to the rescue yet again. With no hesitation he said, "I want you to come live with me and my family." I was blown away. I didn't know how to respond. I didn't feel worthy. He had a wife and two daughters and yet he invited me to stay in his home.

I said yes. I met his wife, Tammy, and their two daughters, Tamara and Sarah. They included me in every activity. I ate dinner with the family, watched movies, took drives to the country, and went to church, too. With all the wonderful things I experienced, they gave me my space to fit in. It's as if they came from a different planet. For the first time I got to see everything that I longed for in a solid family. I don't remember eating together with mine because my mom had to work many hours just to take care of our needs. Sure, there were some times we shared a meal, but even then, it was without the man of the house.

The interaction of the girls with their parents was filled with a certain kind of respect that I can only call Godly. It was more than "yes sir" and "no ma'am." It was the demeanor in which they spoke. There was patience and kindness. And wouldn't you know it? There were tons of laughter too. They may not have realized it, but when they asked me at the dinner table if I want more, my answer of "yes" was not just about food. I wanted what they had—reverence for God and respect for each other, compassionate hospitality, loving family. I craved it more and more every day.

For the next six months, I kept reading my Bible. Effort does not take talent, only time and desire. I had the time, I made the time, and I now had an insurmountable desire to find out who God was, why I was here, and where I will go. I was all in!

Tom Goes to Church

Even though I didn't know how this all worked, I knew I wanted to be around people who talked about God and lived their lives by the Word of God. It dawned on me how many people spoke against God and used His name disrespectfully on and off the golf course. My ears were now so tuned and sensitive wherever I was, hearing the name of Jesus profaned now bothered me.

I was surprised to learn through the Scriptures that thousands of years ago the Apostle Paul had to remind a church in Colossae, "But now you must put them all away: anger, wrath, malice, slander, and obscene talk from your mouth" (Colossians 3:8). Christians had to learn to guard their mouths. Today is no different. We have the same opportunity and choice of what comes out of our mouths concerning God. I was being drawn to praising his name.

The Richards took me to Cornerstone Church with a preacher who didn't mince his words. John

Hagee was the preacher, and he preached hard and direct. I needed that. I needed to be told how to live. I wanted direction and to be told NO! I also wanted to learn about what was right.

I felt a little uncomfortable in the beginning because it was so different from going to a Catholic mass. The participation was different. Mr. Hagee spoke from the open Bible while everyone else had their Bibles open too. Being told that I couldn't understand the Bible from my youth was a complete lie.

To my Catholic friends and family and any who might be reading this book right now, please, I beg you, read the Bible. It's God Word to you! Not only will you understand it, but it will change your perspective, your desires, and your eternity if you let it. When I am able to sit down and share the Scriptures to those of the Catholic faith, the response is almost always the same. "Tom, I never knew that."

I learned from the beginning that the Christian church started in Jerusalem, not Rome. The Apostle Peter was the one to give the very first sermon. He spoke to almost a million people that day because they had come from everywhere to celebrate a feast called Pentecost. Peter preached more boldly than even John Hagee when he said, "Men of Israel, hear these words: Jesus of Nazareth, a man attested to you by God with mighty works and wonders and signs that God did through him in your midst, as you yourselves know—this Jesus, delivered up according to the definite plan and foreknowledge of God, you crucified and killed by the hands of lawless men. God raised him up, loosing the pangs of death, because it was not possible for him to be held by it" (Acts 2:22-24).

Now that's preaching! Wait a minute. That's a public putdown. That's a humiliating thing to hear. That's the truth. Jesus explicitly said, "And you will know the truth, and the truth will set you free" (John 8:32). The truth was hearing what Jesus did for mankind—even more, what He did for me personally.

Three thousand people with each one having a soul, listened to Peter as he continued: "'Let all the house of Israel therefore know for certain that God has made him both Lord and Christ, this Jesus whom you crucified.' Now when they heard this they were cut to the heart, and said to Peter and the rest of the apostles, 'Brothers, what shall we do?'" (Acts 2:36-37).

Hearing about God's love and plan to save us through Jesus Christ evokes different responses: "I've heard it before," or jokes and mocking, disbelief, "later," or even anger or tears. But Peter's listeners responded from their hearts: "Brothers, what shall we do?" The Gospel message of what Jesus did softened their hearts to ask.

Peter answered for every person, every time, every place to hear: "Repent and be baptized every one of you in the name of Jesus Christ for the forgiveness of your sins, and you will receive the gift of the Holy Spirit" (Acts 2:38).

Being baptized as a baby was not a choice of mine, but it was something that my parents did for me. I am thankful that they took the time to do something that they thought was important for me. What's strange about reading this is that as I examined the entire Bible from cover to cover I found out that there were no babies baptized, because no babies needed to be. Jesus Himself said in the Scriptures "Let the little children come to me and do not hinder them, for to such belongs the kingdom of heaven" (Matthew 19:14). I was already in a right relationship with God as a baby; Jesus said so.

In the Gospel of Mark, Jesus tells the twelve Apostles, "Whoever believes and is baptized will be saved" (Mark 16:16). Can a baby believe? "And with many other words he bore witness and continued to exhort them, saying, 'Save yourselves from this crooked generation'" (Acts 2:40).

The Lord made it very clear as to what He commanded and to whom. Jesus said, "All authority in heaven and on earth has been given to me. Go therefore and make disciples of all nations, baptizing them in the name of the Father and of the Son and of the Holy Spirit, teaching them to observe all that I have commanded you" (Matthew 28:18-20).

That sermon was a little more than two thousand years ago but the truth remains. They needed to be saved from a perverse generation of decadence—lust, lies, greed, drunkenness, thievery, adultery, gambling, and homosexuality. Sound familiar? Two thousand years later, Peter's message is the same: "Save yourselves from this crooked generation" (Acts 2:40). What was the response to Peter's message? "So those who received his word were baptized, and there were added that day about three thousand souls" (Acts 2:41).

Grownups were baptized, immersed in water. Their faith led them to repent or turn to God to save them. They did! But I had not. I now firmly believed in Jesus Christ. I was in the process of repenting, but I had not yet been baptized for the remission of my sins.

God Sends a Preacher (I Am Saved)

As fate would have it, I happened into a coffee shop right up the street from the range called "The Hill of Beans." I would stop in at least twice a week for lunch. It was there that I met Jenny, who would become the next person of influence in my spiritual search for God. We became friends, and after a few months she invited me to attend church services with her.

There I met Don Willis. He was probably in his 70s. The congregation was about 150 strong. I liked the smaller number of people. There was an immediate intimate feeling. When Don Willis spoke, he quoted Scripture and explained each passage well. I enjoyed digging into the verses of the Bible and could feel God's Word settling into my heart. There was something else. There was no band or choir. Everybody sang together *a cappella*, meaning without instruments. The singing was amazing! It felt right, even more reverent. The Bible tells us to speak to each other "in psalms and hymns and spiritual songs, singing and making melody to the Lord with your heart" (Ephesians 5:19).

I continued working at the range, spending more time with Jenny, and devouring the Scriptures. The more I read the four Gospels of Matthew, Mark, Luke, and John, the greater I saw how much Jesus Christ loves me personally. He lived to serve His Father in heaven by serving every person he met. He went everywhere teaching the men and women who would listen, telling them that He is the Son of God. He would go on to tell us all that if we want to know what God is like, we need not look any further than Jesus Himself. He taught the masses about who would be blessed. He healed the sick of various diseases and disorders. He made the blind to see. He made the lame to walk. He cured leprosy with one touch. He even brought the dead back to life.

It's easy to see why the Bible is the bestselling book in the world. It is God's Word to man about the past, present, and future. It's God's letter to the world telling us who we are, why we are here, and where we are going. But more than that, it tells us all that there is a loving God Who is so close to us all. He wants all men to know Him and to want to be with Him in heaven. He wants all men everywhere to repent and come to Him. "The times of ignorance God overlooked, but now he commands all people everywhere to repent" (Acts 17:30).

I began noticing in the Bible stories I was reading how many people retreated from Jesus as He spoke. The Lord often spoke about the cost of following Him, the cost of discipleship. One day Jesus was speaking to the multitudes, and suddenly they got up and walked away. One by one they turned their backs on the Lord, basically saying, "It's not worth it."

"So Jesus said to the twelve, 'Do you want to go away as well?' Simon Peter answered him, 'Lord, to whom shall we go? You have the words of eternal life'" (John 6:67-68).

In the Gospel of John, Jesus uses some descriptive terms that the average man can understand WHO He is to each one of us. He said, "I am the door. If anyone enters by me, he will be saved and will go in and out and find pasture" (John 10:9). He also said, "I am the way, and the truth, and the life. No one comes to the Father but through me" (John 14:6). The power of these words convinced me that if I was ever going to go to heaven, it wasn't going to be about whether I did more good things than bad. It was going to be whether I followed this man, the Son of Man, the Son of God! To try any other path was truly gambling with God.

One of the most difficult aspects of reading the Bible wasn't my inability to understand it; rather it was the challenge of applying to my own life. Jesus convinced me that it was not religion that he wanted me to have; it was a relationship. *How was I going to have this relationship with God the Father when I didn't even know how to have a relationship with my earthly father?*

I learned that, "With God all things are possible" (Matthew 19:26). All my life, I had been told that Jesus died for the sins of the world. I always took that to mean that everyone was going to heaven. It doesn't mean that at all; it means that everyone has the opportunity to have their sins taken away because His death on the cross is effective enough to wash away all of man's sins. But every person must believe this and do what Jesus says to do to be saved. To be saved is to be brought safely through, from eternal death to eternal life. The cross of Christ is the one event that every person who has ever lived needs to understand, appreciate, and respond to in order to be saved from death and brought to life.

The story of the cross started long before Christ walked on the earth as a man. When God sent the plagues to the land of Egypt to rescue the children of Israel from Pharaoh, His last plague was the harshest of all. He sent an angel of death to take the life of every firstborn male child in Egypt. Moses instructed God's chosen people to kill an unblemished lamb and take the blood and smear it on the doorposts of the house. When God saw it, He passed over that house. If there was no blood, He went in and killed the firstborn of that family.

Jesus is the Lamb of God, the unblemished lamb. Jesus the Lamb was not sacrificed *to* God, but sacrificed *from* God. Everyone that follows Him and obeys Him has the blood of the Lamb smeared on the doorposts of their souls. This brings them safely through death! I read the Gospel accounts of how they scourged him with whips that had hooks on the end of them to rip the flesh from his back. Here was an innocent man being tortured before going to a cross that He did not deserve. At the cross He suffered a slow death with four large nails piercing His hands and feet.

Reading the account of the crucifixion for the first time had a profound effect on me. I felt sickened for Him. It was not fair at all. He had done nothing wrong and everything right. When I realized that my personal sins were part of the cross of Jesus, it brought me to my knees. His death was now affecting my life! And now I knew that my death would be affected by His death.

What Jesus said while hanging on the cross is forever etched in my mind. "Father, forgive them, for they know not what they do" (Luke 23:34).

I now believed in one major thing, one person in my life—His name is Jesus Christ, the Son of God. I wanted to go to heaven and spend eternity with Him. I wanted to know how to get there and what I had to do.

Don Willis asked if we could have a Bible study together. I agreed, and we met at his house. He wanted to show me a pattern in the Bible from the book of Acts that taught someone what they needed to do to be saved. I had told him I had read Acts 2:38: "Repent and be baptized every one of you in the name of Jesus Christ for the forgiveness of your sins, and you will receive the gift of the Holy Spirit." Mr. Willis asked me what I thought of this. I said that I had been baptized as a baby, but that I had seen adults being baptized at Cornerstone Church. I was confused, not knowing what to think, especially because they had said that baptism is an outward sign of an inward feeling, meaning a person gets baptized to show that they are a Christian already and that baptism has nothing to do with salvation.

Mr. Willis took me through the whole book of Acts to see what baptism was all about. I couldn't wait to find the truth. I knew that whatever the Bible said to do, I would do. He presented to story of the Apostle Paul and his conversion. Paul used to be called Saul. He was part of the Sanhedrin council and a Pharisee. He knew the Law of Moses front and back. He studied under the feet of Gamaliel and was dead set against the followers of Jesus Christ.

One day, Saul was traveling to Damascus to drag Christ-followers off to prison when suddenly he was met there by none other than Jesus Christ Himself. Jesus said to him, *"Saul, Saul, why are you persecuting Me?"*

"Who are you, Lord?" Saul answered.

"I am Jesus of Nazareth."

Saul asked Jesus, *"What shall I do, Lord?"*

"Rise, and go into Damascus, and there you will be told all that is appointed for you to do!" (Acts 22:7-10).

For three days and nights Saul was in Damascus praying, fasting, and blind. He was blind because of the brilliant light of Glory in meeting the resurrected Jesus. In the meantime, God spoke to one of his disciples named Ananias and told him to go to Saul. Ananias pleaded with God that this man Saul was God's enemy. God assured Ananias that this was the right thing to do. Therefore, Ananias went to Saul and told him that he would suffer many things because of the name of Jesus Christ; and then told him these words: "'And now why do you wait? Rise and be baptized and wash away your sins, calling on his name"" (Acts 22:16).

Saul had believed and was now ready to obey. Saul did what he was told to do to have his sins washed away. First Peter told the masses of people, then Ananias told one man what to do—and they were exactly the same.

I started to think about being told that baptism was just an outward sign of an inward feeling. It had nothing to do with an outward sign that I was already a Christian!

How do I or anyone else know this? Because Ananias told Saul that being baptized would wash away his sins! Even though Saul called Him Lord, and fasted and prayed, he was not saved! How do we know? Ananias, on the authority of Almighty God said so when he said, "Why do you wait?" He wasn't saying, "You need to do this as a sign that you are a Christian." He is saying, "You need to do this to wash away your sins!"

The fog of doubt quickly disappeared in my heart. It was now easy to see that there was a big difference in saying that I believed in Jesus Christ and believing enough by faith to do what He says. Saul could have said, "Ananias, I believe in Jesus; isn't that enough?" A man who believes in Jesus, wanting to repent (the way Peter instructed on the day of Pentecost) but not having been baptized, is someone still in their sins. They haven't been brought safely through to be saved. In case there was any last thread of doubt, what I was about to read in Acts 8 would cut that last thread.

Mr. Willis had us read the account of a man named Philip and an Ethiopian eunuch in Acts. The angel of the Lord told Philip to go to the road in the south, the desert in Gaza. There was a man who was reading about the death of Christ from the book of Isaiah. This man was sitting in a chariot and reading to himself. An angel of the Lord told Philip to run and overtake the chariot. Not in anger, but to help this man find the truth. He asked the eunuch, "Do you understand what you are reading?"

The eunuch answered, "How can I, unless someone guides me?"

They started at the Scripture the eunuch was reading (Isaiah 53):

"'Like a sheep he was led to the slaughter and like a lamb before its shearer is silent, so he opens not his mouth. In his humiliation justice was denied him. Who can describe his generation? For his life is taken away from the earth.'" (Acts 8:32-33).

And then Philip preached Jesus to him. The very next line blew me away: "They came to some water, and the eunuch said, 'See, here is water! What prevents me from being baptized?' And he commanded the chariot to stop, and they both went down into the water, Philip and the eunuch, and he baptized him. And when they came up out of the water, the Spirit of the Lord carried Philip away, and the eunuch saw him no more, and went on his way rejoicing" (Acts 8:26-39).

New Testament Conversions

HEARD GOSPEL	BELIEVED	REPENTED	CONFESSED	WERE BAPTIZED	SAVED FROM PAST SINS
Jews on Pentecost Acts 2:1-47		Repented Acts 2:38		Baptized Acts 2:38, 41	Sins Remitted Acts 2:38, 41
Samaritans Acts 8:5-12	Believed Acts 8:12			Baptized Acts 8:12	Saved Mark 16:16
Simon Acts 8:13	Believed Acts 8:13			Baptized Acts 8:13	Saved Mark 16:16
Ethiopian Eunuch Acts 8:26-39	Believed Acts 8:37		Confessed Acts 8:37/Rom 9:10	Baptized Acts 8:38	"Went on His Way Rejoicing" Acts 8:39
Saul Acts 9:1-18; 22:1-16; 26			Confessed Acts 22:10	Baptized Acts 22:16	Sins Washed Away Acts 22:16
Cornelius Acts 10:1-48; 11:1-18	Believed Acts 15:7	Repented Acts 11:18		Baptized Acts 10:48	Saved Acts 11:14
Lydia Acts 16:1-14-15				Baptized Acts 16:15	Saved Acts 16:14-15
Philippian Jailor Acts 16:1-25-34	Believed Acts 16:31-34	Repented Acts 16:33		Baptized Acts 16:33	"Rejoiced" Acts 16:34
Corinthians Acts 18:1-8	Believed Acts 18:8			Baptized Acts 18:8	Washed - Saved 1 Cor. 6:11; 15:2
Ephesians Acts 19:1-7				Baptized Acts 19:5	Redeemed - Saved Eph. 1:7; 2:8

HEARING + BELIEF + REPENTANCE + CONFESSION + BAPTISM = SALVATION FROM PAST SINS

Notice in the chart above: The words believed, repented, and confessed don't always appear. But everyone who heard the Gospel was baptized.

Mr. Willis took me to the end of the book of Matthew. Jesus met with all His disciples back in Jerusalem. It was there that He said to them, "'All authority in heaven and on earth has been given to me. Go therefore and make disciples of all nations, baptizing them in the name of the Father and of the Son and of the Holy Spirit, teaching them to observe all that I have commanded you'" (Matthew 28:18-20). The account in the book of Mark is similar but even more straightforward "'Whoever believes and is baptized will be saved, but whoever does not believe will be condemned'" (Mark 16:16).

It was now very obvious to me. It's as if Jesus was saying to my heart, "Tom, Tom, why do you keep ignoring Me? Why are you waiting?" I was given sign after sign, Scripture after Scripture. The impact of these verses was like throwing a small pebble in a brook and watching the ripples spread. Throw a big rock and watch a big splash. What I had just read was like someone cutting off Rhode Island and throwing it into the ocean. My choice was simple; the answer I had been looking for all my life was right in front of me.

"Let's go right now, Mr. Willis! I want to be baptized in the name of Jesus Christ for the remission of my sins." Just an hour later I became a Christian. I couldn't wait to be baptized. We made a few phone calls and headed straight to the church, and I was baptized that very day.

I became just like Saul (later changed to Paul), just like the 3,000 on the day of Pentecost, and just like the eunuch who believed Jesus and did what he says. The depth of what Christ did for me is more than I can sometimes comprehend. The Bible says that He redeemed me with His precious blood (1 Peter 1:19). He washed me clean (Hebrews 10:22). He transformed me by the renewing of my mind (Romans 12:2). He saved me from the day of wrath. My name was now written in God's Book of Life (Revelation 13:8). I was added to His church (Acts 2:47). "For as many of you as were baptized into Christ have put on Christ" (Galatians 3:27).

I just put on Christ! I am saved, finally a Christian having peace with God. No more dreams about what life is all about. No more worries about being more good than bad, no more fear of death. I finally understand why I was born and happily know where I will spend all eternity—with Jesus Christ, my Lord, my God, my Savior.

The Gospel message of Jesus Christ coming down from heaven to become like a man, yet without sin is the most important truth to man. I now knew that not only was I a sinner and that "all have sinned and fall short of the glory of God" (Romans 3:23) but, I was now a forgiven sinner! He, Jesus Christ, is the only way. His is the only name that matters to a man's soul. His dying a merciless death to take away my sin or your sin is what matters most. Jesus' death, burial and resurrection is the Gospel, and I had just found and obeyed it too!

After putting on Christ in baptism, my old life seemed to simply fall off, one sinful piece at a time. The Apostle Paul explained it perfectly when he reminded the Christians in Ephesus, "And you were dead in the trespasses and sins in which you once walked, following the course of this world, following the prince of the power of the air, the spirit that is now at work in the sons of disobedience—among whom we all once lived in the passions of our flesh, carrying out the desires of the body and the mind, and were by nature children of wrath, like the rest of mankind" (Ephesians 2:1-3).

Chapter 🎲🎲

Breeder's Cup: The Moment of Truth

Four years later, with the "new" man still emerging and the "old" man dying daily, my life was at peace. With my wife and two daughters by my side and God in my heart and mind, I never anticipated such a temptation as this. I thought this particular layer of sin had been peeled away for good. It had not.

It was Breeder's Cup Day, and I had found myself at a crossroads. Would I return to my old ways and place a bet, or would I keep my eyes on Jesus Christ and the new life he was creating in me? My heart pounding and Retama Park quickly approaching, I had closed my eyes. When driving seventy miles per hour, closing your eyes is the last thing you want to do. I did not want to visually see the race track—or crash, but my eyes stayed shut. I said to God, "Please don't let me turn into this place!" I kept driving straight. Praise God! He had made an escape for me (1 Corinthians 10:13).

His Story Became Mine

A tired and angry New York bartender finding the truth about himself through the people at the bar might seem a strange path to encountering God, but that's the way it happened for me. Billy Joel's famous line from "Piano Man" says, "We were sharing a drink they call loneliness, but it's better than drinking alone." When I think of Barry, I will remember that he was a reflection of me as someone lonely who had trouble letting go of the past. When I see Rocky, I see myself as the gambler who needed to stop or else I could end up with my head in an oven too. Perhaps Ms. Fur Coat helped me the most of the three at the bar. Her desire to be loved and understood was mine as well. She wanted to be loved like the rest of us, but often the way we go about it is from a sense of desperation. Their stories became mine.

I was desperate, lonely, and addicted to all the wrong things; and yet, without seeing myself in all three, I might never have yelled in God's direction on that cold winter's night. I clenched my fist at God, but He showed me the hands of His Son. I raised my voice, and He spoke to me through His servants Charlie, Michael, and Don Willis. Before Christ I could forgive no one. With Christ, I can forgive all. I knew nothing about love, and then He showed me the cross. He speaks to my heart through His Word. Now I speak to you, my friends, my family, to your hearts. Are you gambling with God like I was?

Do you know the Savior of the world? One day we will all die. "And just as it is appointed for man to die once, and after that comes judgment" (Hebrews 9:27). Each moment that goes by is another moment closer to that day. Do you remember the days of parking meters? You put a couple of quarters in the meter and got a few hours. When time ran out, the red "expired" sign popped up for all to see. Likewise, when your heart runs out of beats and your time winds down, the expired sign will be placed on your tombstone. What will it say? You will probably be in a cemetery plenty of times in your lifetime, viewing the tombstones of your loved ones. And one day the tombstone will be yours. What if the tombstones read "saved" or "LOST?" What would yours say?

Let me ask you another way: Are you saved? Will you be brought safely through the way God brought Noah and his family through? Are you willing to be led through by Jesus Christ the way Moses led the children of Israel safely through the Red Sea to the eventual promised land? If you are, He has promised to lead you to His promised land; it's called heaven. A Gospel preacher in Houston, Texas, said it best: "If you miss heaven, you've missed all there is."

Jesus saved me! I pray that you will let him save you too! Will His story be yours? Please don't gamble with God.

Now that you have heard my story, I want to talk with you about yours.

I have been a Born Again Christian for about nineteen years. I am a minister at the church where I attend. When I say minister, I mean servant. God has put it into my heart to minister to other's needs. If that is you, then I am pleased to help in any and all ways. The object of this book is to help you to see the truth about Almighty God and His Son Jesus Christ.

He tells all "But when one turns to the Lord, the veil is removed" (2 Corinthians 3:16). People's eyes are covered and blind and without God in this world. When someone like you or me turn to the Lord, that veil, the blindness, is removed. You or anyone else will now be able to see the answers to the age-old question of "Why was I born?"

Most of us are raised to think that life consists of the things we accumulate. "Live life to the fullest," we're told. "Settle down, have some kids, retire, become a grandparent, and eventually die." All the while we assume that living a productive life, being a decent human being, and paying taxes are enough to get us to heaven.

My friend, this just isn't true. Solomon, the wisest man who ever lived, says this, "He has put eternity into man's heart" (Ecclesiastes 3:11). Solomon goes on to say, "The end of the matter; all has been heard. Fear God and keep his commandments, for this is the whole duty of man. For God will bring every deed into judgment, with every secret thing, whether good or evil" (Ecclesiastes 12:13-14). Being productive, having kids, and living a moral life are all well and good, but there's so much more. God has put eternity in our hearts so that we will seek Him and accept the gift of His salvation through Jesus Christ.

Are you saved? As my brother Charlie said, "When you don't know, you know!"

Then What?

You are born. **Then what?**

You become a child. **Then what?**

You go to grade school, middle school, high school. **Then what?**

You graduate and go to college. **Then what?**

You get your degree and start looking for a career that will pave the way for your future. **Then what?**

You get that perfect job. **Then what?**

You get serious about the one you're dating and decide to marry. **Then what?**

You begin your new life together. **Then what?**

You have a baby. You eventually have two more. They are growing. You are parenting. You laugh, you cry, you spend each day living the American Dream. **Then what?**

Time flies and the last child leaves for college. **Then what?**

You're both still young. You're successful as parents and have good careers. The mortgage is just about paid off. The retirement accounts are in place. You take vacations and learn new hobbies. **Then what?**

You go to your children's weddings. The family grows. You love being grandparents. You take the grandkids for the weekend. You talk about all the great memories of your happy, healthy family. **Then what?**

You retire. Your working life is now over. You try to figure out what to do next. **Then what?**

It seems that more of your high school and college friends are passing away. You attend more funerals each year. You start to question your own mortality. **Then what?**

Fatigue sets in. You sleep less. Your hair is white or gone. Your walk is slow. Aches and pains are a normal day of life. **Then what?**

You feel unimportant. **Then what?**

It might be cancer, a prolonged illness, or your heart might give out. **Then what?**

You are dead. **Then what?**

Your eternal life is in the hands of God!

The second half of this book is dedicated to helping you turn to God so he can answer that question, **"Then what?"**

Part Two

Then What?

The following pages represent my sincere concern for your soul. The love, mercy, and grace of God encompass the most precious commodity of all—forgiveness. This is what's at stake. God has led me to this moment of sharing some truths that might be difficult to hear.

"The Lord is not slow to fulfill his promise as some count slowness, but is patient toward you, not wishing that any should perish, but that all should reach repentance" (2 Peter 3:9).

The Lord's warning is part of his grace, mercy, love, and forgiveness. He desires that none should perish, but that all would come to Him.
Come to Him, my friend.

Chapter ⚃⚃

Finding Freedom

I met with ten Mexican Mafia members at a local prison one afternoon. I told them, "I spent twenty-five years in prison."

They looked at me in shock, as if to say, "No way, bro." I hesitated another second or two before telling them that my prison bars were between my ears. I was held captive in my life and mind to things like gambling, hate, sexual immorality, and lying. I was even afraid to go to funerals. Friend, read this for yourself. Through death, Jesus "might destroy the one who has the power of death, that is, the devil, and deliver all those who through fear of death were subject to lifelong slavery" (Hebrews 2:14-15). Until I encountered God, I'd been subject to bondage and fear.

To someone in the Mexican Mafia or to an atheist that might not mean a thing. Someone doesn't get to be in the Mafia or get to a place of believing God doesn't exist without a lack of fear. For the Mafia member, he needs to be a man. Most have never had a real man, a father figure, to help them out when they were young. Gang members are often looking for someone to cling to. The closeness of a gang sometimes runs deeper and with more commitment than some of the friendships and marriages of everyday people. Not only will a gang member take a bullet for his friend, but he will deliver one to anyone who dares to cross him or a member. His devotion says, "I have no fear of man or even of death." This is what the gang member believes, but it is a lie. Scripture says God has "put eternity into man's heart" (Ecclesiastes 3:11).

I asked the men, "Do you all believe that you're going to die one day? If so, please raise your hand." All hands went up.

"Do you all believe in God?" Every hand went up except for one.

I put away my Bible and asked the man what his name was. "Thomas," he said.

"That's my name, too. Do you mind if I share a story with you?"

He listened. I told him, "Picture this: You get out of prison, and you and I become great friends for the next forty years. One day we are hanging out in a park eating and talking when someone comes up to us and says, 'Guys, this is your last day on earth. You are both going to die later today.'"

I looked Thomas in the eyes and asked, "Do you know what the difference between us is?" His eyes were glued to me. "The difference is, I am going to die with hope and you are going to die in fear. I have everything to look forward to and you do not." He smiled sheepishly. I knew he understood the story. Perhaps it was the first time for him to have real thoughts or fears about his mortality.

Thomas was not only a Mexican Mafia gang member; he was also an atheist. I believe Thomas and all atheists are all connected by the fact that they haven't tasted the Word of God. They haven't been told about Jesus Christ. Or if they have, they want to believe they can avoid His name, His way, and His judgment. The Word of God tells the truth. Here it is. "The one who rejects me and does not receive my words has a judge; the word that I have spoken will judge him on the last day" (John 12:48).

"And just as it is appointed for man to die once, and after that comes judgment" (Hebrews 9:27). If by chance this describes you, then I know that you are gambling your soul with God. It's not too late while you're on this side of the grave. May God grant you enough days to call out to him to be saved.

Reasons People Don't Turn to God

"God Can't Forgive Me!"

Some years ago, I was giving golf lessons to a man named Andy. He refused my invitation to come to church services. "God could never forgive me for some of the things I have done in this life," Andy said.

Jesus taught a lesson on this very subject. He said in the Gospel of Luke, "'A certain moneylender had two debtors. One owed five hundred denarii, and the other fifty. When they could not pay, he cancelled the debt of both. Now which of them will love him more?' Simon answered, 'The one, I suppose, for whom he cancelled the larger debt.' And he said to him, 'You have judged rightly.'" Jesus goes on to say, 'Therefore I tell you, her sins, which are many, are forgiven—for she loved much. But he who is forgiven little, loves little'" (Luke 7:41-43, 47).

The Bible tells us it is hard for a rich man to go to heaven because he trusts in riches. It is the poor who have an easier time believing in the Lord. Likewise, perhaps it is those who have sinned the most or at least have lived a life of doing many things contrary to the will of God who are most likely to become Christians and who are also the ones who will serve him the most. Why? Because they have been forgiven much; they understand his gift of forgiveness. To all the Andys of the world: If Jesus can save the Apostle Paul, who was guilty of persecuting the very church that Jesus had died for, then he can forgive your sins too.

If you believe, "God can't forgive me," consider this perspective on those four words:

God—You speak his name therefore you believe that he is God!

Can't—If he can't then,

- No one can.
- What kind of God would this be to serve anyway?

Forgive—Isn't the person uttering these words begging to be forgiven?

Me—You're saying that God can forgive everyone except you.

Stay with me. Think about these four words another way. Instead of saying He can't, rearrange the words in the form of a question: "Can't God forgive me?" If you can humble yourself to ask, He will bring you to the answer—yes! Jesus said it best on the cross: "Father, forgive them, for they know not what they do" (Luke 23:34).

Let's try another combination: "God forgive me!"

If and when you come to this point, you are moments away from having your sins washed away by His blood. Seconds away from having your name written in the Lamb's Book of Life.

If you now believe that Jesus Christ is the Son of God who came to this earth to save souls, you are now ready to die with Him. What the Apostle Peter told them to do at Pentecost is what I tell you to do today: "Repent and be baptized every one of you in the name of Jesus Christ for the forgiveness of your sins" (Acts 2:38).

God can and wants to forgive you!

My friend, what have you done that God can't forgive you? Would you gamble your soul's eternity that He is not able or willing to when your proof is right here in front of you? May God grant you enough days to choose eternal life and to die with Him, instead of choosing eternal death thinking that God can't forgive you.

"I'll Think About God Later"

You are gambling with God if you are waiting until you have seemingly got everything out of life here on earth before deciding to think about life after death. I've heard it said many times, "I'll think about that later. I'll deal with it at a more appropriate time. I don't have time to think about spiritual things right now." Some might even think they'll wait until the very last second when they are on the death bed. My friend, last rites from a priest will not save you from your sins. I know you have seen it on television or have been told that a priest is going over to a house to administer last rites. With sincere compassion, without ever compromising the truth of God's Word, I tell you that you can't find that in the pages of the Word of God.

The thief who was crucified alongside Christ was saved while taking his last breaths. Thank God that he was being crucified next to the Savior of the world that day! Yes, it is true that this man was saved on his "death bed" (the cross), but I need to share with you why. The thief lived under the old law. Jesus Christ lived under the old law too. Jesus did not give the command to be baptized until after he had died and was resurrected.

The writer of Hebrews explains, "For where a will is involved, the death of the one who made it must be established. For a will takes effect only at death, since it is not in force as long as the one who made it is alive" (Hebrews 9:16-17). The new law did not begin until Jesus Christ died and was resurrected. Jesus didn't give the command on how to be saved until he came back to life and told the Apostles. Simply put, a man can't obey a command that hasn't been given yet; therefore, the thief didn't need to get baptized because Jesus commanded it fifty days later, after the thief had died. Today, Jesus does not say just believe like the thief; instead, He says, "Whoever believes and is baptized will be saved" (Mark 16:16).

Often, Jesus healed people or told them that their sins were washed away. When the thief believed and asked the Lord to remember him, Jesus, seeing his faith and knowing his heart, told him that he would be with Him in paradise later that day. Jesus could save anyone who wanted to be saved when He was teaching and preaching while He was presenting the Gospel of salvation. However, after Jesus Christ died on the cross, He was resurrected and then called the Apostles together to give them what is commonly called the Great Commission, or the way for man to be saved (Matthew 28:19-20): "Go therefore and make disciples of all nations, baptizing them in the name of the Father and of the Son and of the Holy Spirit, teaching them to observe all that I have commanded you." Jesus Christ just gave the command to the Apostles on how to be saved. It is Jesus who saves, not a priest or a person.

I once sat at the bed of a man four days before he died. I asked him, "Do you believe in God?"

He said, "Yes."

"Do you believe in Jesus Christ and that He is the Son of God?"

He again affirmed, "Yes!"

We talked about how he would be meeting God very soon. "Have you been baptized into Christ?" I asked.

When he said that he was baptized as a baby, I explained that babies don't need to be baptized because they are not guilty. He stared at me in disbelief. As he was about to speak, his wife came in the room and our conversation stopped. I will never forget leaving the room and saying goodbye as he turned from his wife and said to me, "I want to talk some more about this with you later."

His wife came out to meet me in the living room twenty minutes later and said, "You are not allowed to go back into that room and speak to him." She said that what I told him made him upset.

With respect, I said to his wife, "This is bigger than you or me. Your husband wants to know what he needs to do to go to heaven."

She told me he was just placating me. I would not be allowed back in his room. He died a few days later.

Jesus said what was required for salvation, the Apostles taught it, and I simply want to give you the same message.

Don't be shocked when you read it for yourself that the Apostle Peter told the first three thousand people who believed in Jesus what they needed to do to be saved.

They asked Peter, "What shall we do?"

Peter could have said, "Nothing. You guys believe—that's good enough for me." He could have said, "Just repent (turn to God) and that will be acceptable to him." But he didn't. He said, "Repent and be baptized every one of you in the name of Jesus Christ for the forgiveness of your sins" (Acts 2:38). He, the Apostle Peter, the one who walked with Jesus for three years said it. What right or "rite" do I or any other preacher have in telling you something less or different from the very words of our Savior Jesus Christ?

Will you be persuaded? Or are you going to take that gamble with God by dying without looking into the pages of God's Word? Will you tell God that you thought you would have more time and would think about it later? Or that you were planning on doing it when you were on your death bed?

My friend, are the world's ways of life so satisfying that you have no time to think about your own mortality?

We read in the book of Acts about the day the Apostle Paul went to speak with a king named Agrippa. He asked the king, "Do you believe the prophets?" Paul answered his own question before the king had a chance. "I know that you believe."

Paul knew Agrippa believed the Messiah (Jesus) was coming: the king's answer may be even more common today: "In a short time would you persuade me to be a Christian?" (Acts 26:27-28).

There is a song from the 1800s still sung today that tears at the believer's heart.

"Almost Persuaded" by Philip Paul Bliss

"Almost persuaded" now to believe;
"Almost persuaded" Christ to receive;
Seems now some soul to say,
"Go, Spirit, go Thy way,
Some more convenient day
On Thee I'll call."

"Almost persuaded," come, come today;
"Almost persuaded," turn not away;
Jesus invites you here,
Angels are ling'ring near,
Prayers rise from hearts so dear;
O wand'rer, come!

"Almost persuaded," harvest is past!
"Almost persuaded," doom comes at last!
"Almost" cannot avail;
"Almost" is but to fail!
Sad, sad, that bitter wail—
"Almost," but lost!

My friend, if your heart feels tugged at, I am happy for you. This song speaks to those on the spiritual fence. As you sit on that fence and look at where you've been you may see many good things. But if you choose to look on the other side, you will see only the best. The invitation from Jesus to come to him to be saved is more than enough. Your soul is infected with the cancer called sin. From the time of Jesus Christ hanging on the cross until this very moment you are reading this, the plan now and from the beginning is for you to spend eternity with God when this short life is over. The destiny that awaits us all is a date with the judgment. That judgment will be with Jesus Christ.

"Almost Persuaded" will always be "Almost, but Lost." Lost means doomed. Doomed means forsaken by God. Forsaken by God means to be judged, to have the sins of your life held against you. Judged means your eternity is spent in a place called hell. Hell is where masses upon masses of people will spend their eternity without God and in the presence of the Devil and his angels. There is wailing and gnashing of teeth. That's real pain. A lifetime of pain. A lifetime that never ends.

Yes, abominable men and women will be there. But residing there also will be nice normal men and women from the twentieth century who paid their taxes in full and on time, who raised a family, who lent a helping hand to their respective community. All the good things that men and women do will carry no weight at the judgment because of one thing—they didn't obey the Gospel of Jesus Christ. They didn't believe that one sin could separate them from God. Perhaps they didn't think that they had ever even committed one sin in their lives. But the Word of God proclaims, "For all have sinned and fall short of the glory of God" (Romans 3:23).

Athletes, entertainers, bankers, teachers, nurses and doctors, uncles and aunts, mothers and fathers, brothers and sisters, grandmothers and grandfathers will be where the worst vile people of the world spend their eternities. Why? Because even though the Hitlers of the world never did get close to ever believing in God, the "Almost Persuaded" people of the world are also deemed unforgiven of their sins. That's where you are, my friend, if you have never obeyed the Gospel.

Finally, a man persuaded not is a man who will be lost for all eternity even though he came so close to the truth, so close to believing. But so close to believing will be perhaps the most agonizing of all people in hell. The day after day torment of knowing, *I was about to respond. I almost did that one day, but I didn't.* These will be the haunting thoughts and screams of the lost who will cry out to God, "Please give me one more chance!" But to no avail. They must have pounded on the door to Noah's ark when the rain came down in buckets. As the level of water rose to enormous heights and their eyes saw that people were drowning, they must have gone to where Noah had been telling them that the flood of all floods was coming. But to no avail. God shut the door that day. All the pounding in the world was not going to open it. All the praying and shouting to God would not be heard.

The flood killed them all because, though some of the people of that day were probably almost persuaded, their story ended in the same way yours will—almost, but lost.

Be saved right now. "And now why do you wait? Rise and be baptized and wash away your sins, calling on his name" (Acts 22:16).

Chapter ⚃⚃

What God Says About Sexual Immorality

I am concerned about you if you are a sexually immoral man or woman: fornicator, adulterer, homosexual. As you read this section, you should know there is forgiveness of sin. If these paragraphs describe you or your past, I pray you will be inspired to come to repentance and find forgiveness in Christ. Just because it's your past, it doesn't have to be your future. With Christ, there is forgiveness and abundant life. You need only to come to Him.

Look around you. Isn't it easy to see? We are a nation of people who have lost the sense of shame and embarrassment. Sexting, pornography, prostitution, sexually transmitted diseases, abortions, and sex trafficking are at an all-time high. We tolerate Spring Break drunkenness; we hand out free condoms and swap sexual partners. Men love men, women love women, and we say this is progress. We say that we are free, when we are a nation that is a slave to a pleasure principle called sex. Have it whenever and with whomever you want, and that is perfectly acceptable by some standards. Some parents even encourage their young adult children to experiment. We are bombarded with advertising revolving strictly around the "sex sells" tactic. God never intended it to be this way.

Fornication is a sin. You may call it sex, love-making, or intercourse. If you are not married, God calls it sin. College students may call it "sowing wild oats" before they get married. If you don't get married, but rather live with somebody while having sexual relations, it is sin. "For you may be sure of this, that everyone who is sexually immoral or impure … has no inheritance in the kingdom of Christ and God. Let no one deceive you with empty words, for because of these things the wrath of God comes upon the sons of disobedience" (Ephesians 5:5-6). Your sin is hanging like a gigantic weight around your shoulders. What are you going to do? I have been in your shoes. I know about that weight. I never thought that I could change my behavior, but God helped me. You can say no. I did. God's power is such that if you want to stop any behavior you can, because God will provide an escape.

Listen to what the Apostle Paul told a group of Christians in a place called Corinth (modern-day Greece). "Or do you not know that the unrighteous will not inherit the kingdom of God? Do not be deceived:

neither the sexually immoral, nor idolaters, nor adulterers, nor men who practice homosexuality, nor thieves, nor the greedy, nor drunkards, nor revilers, nor swindlers will inherit the kingdom of God. And such were some of you. But you were washed, you were sanctified, you were justified in the name of the Lord Jesus Christ and by the Spirit of our God" (1 Corinthians 6:9-11).

Do you see it? The sexually immoral sins of our day are not only in the United States, but all over the world. We pride ourselves and continue to speak what has always been our motto, "One nation under God." However, we are failing in our pursuit.

What God Says About Adultery

Adultery is a sin. There is an obvious and a not-so-obvious form of adultery that I want to bring to your attention. The obvious is a man or woman who has an affair with another's spouse. Here are the typical reasons:

"I don't love him/her anymore."

"I'm bored."

"We don't get along."

"I'm not attracted to this person any longer."

You see, the boredom and attraction is a problem that most people may never learn to overcome through love. We simply have not learned what love truly is. Many see it as a physical thing alone. If that describes you, then you don't love, you lust. Isn't this the reason affairs happen? "The other person can understand me and take care of my sexual needs better than my spouse can." This is a selfish attitude. If there are children involved, they will eventually be hit by this tidal wave of dishonestly and sexual betrayal. The spouse who has been cheated on will be left feeling betrayed. How can they trust again?

This sin, or as I call it, *sleeping with the enemy*, is rampant and glorified in the entertainment industry. The affairs of sports professionals and actors are emblazoned across the news headlines. This flippancy trickles down to mainstream society, to ordinary people. Sadly, even into God's church. The Apostle Paul reminded them that "… such were some of you" but they were washed, sanctified, justified. They were made clean by the blood of Jesus Christ. They were baptized, set apart (sanctified), and justified (made innocent). They were even at times attempting to go back into this lifestyle. Paul had to squash this lifestyle. The sin of adultery is nothing more than wrecking somebody else's marriage and killing your conscience at the same time.

The not-so-obvious form of adultery is not only more prevalent, but it looms in the shadows. I say this because this is not thought of as sinful. What God says is sin, man says is love. I am talking about the man or woman who falls out of love with their spouse and gets a divorce. Then a few years later, they find Mr./Mrs. Right. They can't believe they have now found their soulmate. They go on to get married, have children, and refer to their relationship as being a Godsend. Only they don't know yet that God has not sent His blessing at all.

You see, Jesus spoke specifically about this situation. The sin of adultery in the eyes of Almighty God is attached to those who have divorced their spouses for the wrong reason. Jesus Christ said that there is only one reason for a married couple to divorce and have the right to remarry again. "And I say to you: whoever divorces his wife, except for sexual immorality, and marries another, commits adultery" (Matthew 19:9). According to Jesus Christ Himself, if you divorce your spouse and marry another for any reason other than sexual immorality, you are guilty of adultery.

In the Bible, Jesus meets a woman who had five marriages. Jesus, Who knows everything, asked the woman to call her husband. When she answered, Jesus quickly responded. "You are right in saying, 'I have no husband'; for you have had five husbands, and the one you now have is not your husband. What you have said is true" (John 4:17-18). This woman was guilty of the sin of adultery. She knew it and so did Jesus. If this woman was ever going to be right with God, she would have to end her relationship with this current man. I know this sounds unfair and harsh, but it's the truth.

"The one who conquers will have this heritage, and I will be his God and he will be my son. But as for the cowardly, the faithless, the detestable, as for murderers, the sexually immoral, sorcerers, idolaters, and all liars, their portion will be in the lake that burns with fire and sulfur, which is the second death" (Revelation 21:7-8).

I am telling you this to say, don't gamble with God! This is very serious. Your eternal soul's wellbeing could hinge on whom you marry. If you get a divorce because it just didn't work out and you marry another, God says you are guilty of adultery.

What God Says About Homosexuality

Homosexuality is a sin. To anyone facing this difficult challenge, my heart goes out to you.

Who would have thought that my gambling addiction could be a sin; I certainly didn't. It is not my call to make, it is God's. I certainly don't know your situation of how you came to be homosexual, but I have spoken enough people to understand some of the thoughts behind it. I know of a man who was homosexual and is no longer. I don't know if he is a spiritual man or not. I just know that he is married to a loving wife. I have been told that our bodies have a certain gene that decides whether someone is heterosexual or homosexual. If that is the case, then what happened to the gene of the man that left homosexuality and got married to a woman? I realize that there is an outcry for equality and respect to those who choose to engage in this practice.

My friend, it is with more respect than you can imagine that I say these things to you today. My concern for you is that you have the same opportunity to go to heaven as anyone else. Therefore, may I simply tell you the truth—God says that you can't go to heaven if you live this life as a homosexual. I have an obligation to pass along any and all words that come from God. Before I reveal the specifics of what He says, know this for all time. God loves you and made you in His image (Genesis 1:27). He didn't make any mistakes at your birth. God didn't make a man an alcoholic or a gambler. He didn't make people to speak lies either. Someone else has put a lie into your heart to believe that homosexuality is something you are born with, don't have a choice about, and can't change.

Here are the direct words from Almighty God spoken by and written to those who not only lived a life of homosexuality, but those who had become Christians. "Or do you not know that the unrighteous will not inherit the kingdom of God? Do not be deceived: neither the sexually immoral, nor idolaters, nor adulterers, nor men who practice homosexuality, nor thieves, nor the greedy, nor drunkards, nor revilers, nor swindlers will inherit the kingdom of God. And such were some of you. But you were washed, you were sanctified, you were justified in the name of the Lord Jesus Christ and by the Spirit of our God" (1 Corinthians 6:9-11).

I hope you noticed that the list is very long that includes homosexuality but in no way isolates it as something greater or more sinful than the others mentioned. Please understand that the Apostle Paul has written a letter to the church residing in Corinth. This letter is to Christians. The people that made up that church practiced the very list that you see. I say practiced because they left those practices to become Christians. They used to get drunk on a regular basis, cheat others in money matters, have affairs with another's wife and yes, practice homosexuality. They were all convinced that these practices were sinful against God. But you know what? They were also convinced that once they recognized their practice as sin, they could be forgiven. Paul preached the cross of Christ, the one Who could wash away every sin.

Why then does Paul write this letter to a church believing in Jesus and mention all these practices? Because they were starting to believe that they could do these things in spite of what Jesus did on the cross.

A similar situation was happening in Rome, too. Paul wrote, "What shall we say then? Are we to continue in sin that grace may abound? By no means!" (Romans 6:1-2).

Christians then and now struggle with sinful desires even after becoming Christians. They were told that homosexuality is a sin against God and that they needed to repent and turn to God for forgiveness. That forgiveness is only found in Jesus Christ. With love in his heart and the truth in his hands Paul then reminded them gently by saying, "And such were some of you [drunkards, adulterers, homosexuals]. But you were washed, you were sanctified, you were justified in the name of the Lord Jesus Christ and by the Spirit of our God." (1 Corinthians 6:11). My friend, do you see that what Paul said? "Such were some of you."

You used to live like this, but you were washed clean.

You were cleansed by the blood of Jesus Christ when you were baptized into Christ.

You are set apart to live for God now.

You are no longer guilty for the sins that you have committed all your life.

In a not-so-gentle way, the Apostle Paul wrote a letter to a young preacher named Timothy. Not only did Paul remind him that there would come a time when people would want to have their ears tickled, and they would find preachers who would appease them. People would want to hear only things that made them feel good, nothing that might bother their consciences.

Paul told Timothy, "Now we know that the law is good, if one uses it lawfully, understanding this, that the law is not laid down for the just but for the lawless and disobedient, for the ungodly and sinners, for the unholy and profane, for those who strike their fathers and mothers, for murderers, the sexually immoral, men who practice homosexuality, enslavers, liars, perjurers, and whatever else is contrary to sound doctrine, in accordance with the gospel of the glory of the blessed God with which I have been entrusted" (1 Timothy 1:8-11).

Paul had been entrusted with the words of Almighty God. Neither he nor any other Christian in this world is looking to crucify the homosexual. We all have crucified our Savior with our sins. The Apostle Paul had Christians killed before becoming a Christian himself. Yes, he was guilty of murder. You, my friend, have not murdered but you are sinning by practicing homosexuality. Paul called himself the "foremost" among sinners (1 Timothy 1:15). Will you call your-self a sinner? If so, Jesus can save you the same way He saved Paul and all Christians today.

God says that there are people then and now who don't like to retain Him in their minds and who live as they please without a thought to how God feels about it. Again, in the letter to Timothy, in speaking about a woman, Paul tells Timothy, "But she who is self-indulgent is dead even while she lives" (1 Timothy 5:6). Paul told the church at Rome, "Because they exchanged the truth about God for a lie and worshiped and served the creature rather than the Creator, who is blessed forever! Amen. For this reason God gave them up to dishonorable passions. For their women exchanged natural relations for those that are contrary to nature; and the men likewise gave up natural relations with women and were consumed with passion for one another, men committing shameless acts with men and receiving in themselves the due penalty for their error. And since they did not see fit to acknowledge God, God gave them up to a debased mind to do what ought not to be done" (Romans 1:25-28).

My friend, have you been believing a lie that goes way back in time? Why do you think people still refer to Sodom and Gomorrah? God was not so long-suffering then. The entire region was destroyed because of homosexuality. Under the old law, if someone practiced homosexuality, they were stoned to death. "If a man lies with a male as with a woman, both of them have committed an abomination; they shall surely be put to death; their blood is upon them" (Leviticus 20:13). What God says in the New Testament should offer some hope. "The Lord is not slow to fulfill his promise as some count slowness, but is patient toward you, not wishing that any should perish, but that all should reach repentance" (2 Peter 3:9).

My friend, if you are struggling with this sin I understand the pain and suffering. If you are dead set on this lifestyle and dismiss everything I have just written to you, then I am more worried for you than the one who is struggling. God is longsuffering for sure, but you don't know the day of your last breath here on earth. God can and will change the desires of your flesh if you want him to; he is that loving. If you still resist, then I must say what Paul said, "Therefore, knowing the fear of the Lord, we persuade others" (2 Corinthians 5:11).

Paul then, and I now, have attempted to persuade you knowing the terror of the Lord. That terror will be at the judgment. Please, please, I beg you to turn from this and any other sin into the loving arms of Jesus Christ. He can make you whole again. Maybe, just maybe you will be the one to write the next book, your story. May God give you enough days of life on this earth to make the most important decision of your life in becoming a child of God.

Please don't gamble with God!

What God Says About "The Sinner's Prayer"

If you have been told by your preacher/pastor to come down to the front to receive Christ then you went to the front of the church and prayed a prayer that goes something like this: "Dear God, I repent of my sins. I ask you to come into my heart; I make you the Lord of my life." I want you to know that I understand why you did this. By that I mean that if you did say those words to God then I can assume that your heart is searching for truth. There is no doubt in my opinion that for you to make such a declaration then you are wanting to know God and His Son Jesus Christ.

May I tell you the truth? I said the same things once, too. However, I had not heard from any preacher or pastor on what I needed to do. I simply fell to my knees and asked God to help me. He did! He brought people into my life to bring the Word of God into my heart. Well, here it is. I am concerned for you if you said this prayer believing that you are now saved.

Why would I say such a thing? Because I have searched the Scriptures for the last twenty years and have not found anyone in the New Testament after the resurrection of Jesus Christ to say this prayer to be saved. I will let you decide what the truth is by showing you a comparison of what Jesus Christ Himself said followed by the Apostle Peter, then what the preacher told the future Apostle Paul to do and finally some famous preachers of today.

See and read for yourselves what you need to do to be saved:

The Holy Bible: Read these verses over and over until you know them by heart!		Preachers: Compare what these famous preachers say with what the Bible says.	
Jesus Christ	"Whoever believes and is baptized will be saved" (Mark 16:16).	Billy Graham	"Believe on the Lord Jesus Christ and you will be saved."
Apostle Peter	"Repent and be baptized every one of you in the name of Jesus Christ for the forgiveness of your sins" (Acts 2:38).	Charles Stanley	"Accept (or receive) Jesus Christ as Lord and Savior and put your trust in Him."
Paul's Conversion	"And now why do you wait? Rise and be baptized and wash away your sins, calling on his name" (Acts 22:16).	Joel Osteen	"Pray this prayer: 'Dear Lord, I repent of my sins. I ask you to come into my heart and I make you the Lord of my life.'" Mr. Osteen goes on to say, "Everyone who stood up by faith this morning has just been washed in the blood of Jesus."
Eunuch's Conversion	"See, here is water! What prevents me from being baptized?" (Acts 8:36).		

Question: What does your preacher preach? How does he invite someone to become a Christian? Are you saved? Have you followed the preaching from the Bible or the preaching from man? The famous preachers are preaching truth, but is it the whole truth? What are the preachers missing? Baptism! Read it for yourselves; you do not have to take my word for it.

What God Says About Baptism

- "Whoever believes and is **baptized** will be saved" (Mark 16:16).

- "Repent and be **baptized** every one of you in the name of Jesus Christ for the forgiveness of your sins" (Acts 2:38).

- "And now why do you wait? Rise and be **baptized** and wash away your sins, calling on his name" (Acts 22:16).

- "For as many of you as were **baptized** into Christ have put on Christ" (Galatians 3:27).

- "See, here is water! What prevents me from being **baptized**?" (Acts 8:36).

- "Do you not know that all of us who have been **baptized** into Christ Jesus were **baptized** into his death?" (Romans 6:3).

- "But when they believed Philip as he preached good news about the kingdom of God and the name of Jesus Christ, they were **baptized**, both men and women. Even Simon himself believed, and after being **baptized** he continued with Philip" (Acts 8:12-13).

- "Can anyone withhold water for **baptizing** these people, who have received the Holy Spirit just as we have?" And he commanded them to be **baptized** in the name of Jesus Christ" (Acts 10:47-48).
- "Go therefore and make disciples of all nations, **baptizing** them in the name of the Father and of the Son and of the Holy Spirit" (Matthew 28:18-19).
- "**Baptism**, which corresponds to this, now saves you, not as a removal of dirt from the body but as an appeal to God for a good conscience" (1 Peter 3:21).
- "Jesus answered him, 'Truly, truly, I say to you, unless one is born again he cannot see the kingdom of God.' Nicodemus said to him, 'How can a man be born when he is old? Can he enter a second time into his mother's womb and be born?' Jesus answered, 'Truly, truly, I say to you, unless one is **born of water** and the Spirit, he cannot enter the kingdom of God.'" (John 3:3-5)

Many of today's most influential preachers leave out the step of baptism. Jesus and Paul and Peter did not.

"And as they were going along the road they came to some water, and the eunuch said, 'See, here is water! What prevents me from being baptized?'" - Acts 8:36

"But when they believed Philip as he preached good news about the kingdom of God and the name of Jesus Christ, they were baptized, both men and women." - Acts 8:12

"And Peter said to them, 'Repent and be baptized every one of you in the name of Jesus Christ for the forgiveness of your sins, and you will receive the gift of the Holy Spirit.'" - Acts 2:38

"And he commanded them to be baptized in the name of Jesus Christ." - Acts 10:48

"And Jesus came and said to them, 'All authority in heaven and on earth has been given to me. Therefore, go and make disciples of all the nations, baptizing them in the name of the Father and the Son and the Holy Spirit.'" - Matthew 28:18-19

"And now why do you wait? Rise and be baptized and wash away your sins, calling on his name." - Acts 22:16

"Whoever believes and is baptized will be saved, but whoever does not believe will be condemned." - Mark 16:16

"Do you not know that all of us who have been baptized into Christ Jesus were baptized into his death? We were buried therefore with him by baptism into death, in order that, just as Christ was raised from the dead by the glory of the Father, we too might walk in newness of life." - Romans 6:3-4

"For as many of you as were baptized into Christ have put on Christ." - Gal 3:27

"having been buried with him in baptism, in which you were also raised with him through faith in the powerful working of God, who raised him from the dead." - Col 2:12

BAPTISM SAVES!

"And they said, 'Believe in the Lord Jesus, and you will be saved, you and your household.' And they spoke the word of the Lord to him and to all who were in his house. And he took them the same hour of the night and washed their wounds; and he was baptized at once, he and all his family." - Acts 16:31-33

"Baptism, which corresponds to this, now saves you, not as a removal of dirt from the body but as an appeal to God for a good conscience, through the resurrection of Jesus Christ," - 1 Peter 3:21

What Man Says About Baptism

"Baptism is an outward sign of an inward feeling." *Can you find a verse that says that?*

"Baptism is not necessary for salvation." *Peter says "Baptism now saves you" (1 Peter 3:21).*

"Baptism is a work." *Yes! It is a work, not of man, but of Almighty God (Colossians 2:12).*

"Baptism in the Bible is Holy Spirit baptism not water." *Ask Paul, Cornelius, and 3,000 on Pentecost.*

"Baptism is for babies." *There is not one passage of a baby/child being baptized.*

"Baptism is optional." *Read the Book and decide for yourself.*

Half-truths began back in Genesis, the first book of the Bible. "But the serpent said to the woman, 'You will not surely die. For God knows that when you eat of it your eyes will be opened, and you will be like God, knowing good and evil'" (Genesis 3:4-5). Similarly, when it comes to baptism, many half-truths are spoken.

Wouldn't it just be like the devil of old to say to people today who are trying to obey God that they will be saved even if they do not get baptized? Jesus says, "Whoever believes and is baptized will be saved" (Mark 6:16).

There is no doubt that we must accept Him as Savior. Of course, we do. If He is not Savior, then there is no saving to be done. And yes, we must put our trust in Him for what He did on the cross for our sins. The Bible says, "He became the source of eternal salvation to all who obey him" (Hebrews 5:9). Jesus gave the Great Commission after He was resurrected from the grave. He got the Apostles together and told them exactly what he wanted them to teach and preach. He said, "Go therefore and make disciples of all nations, baptizing them in the name of the Father and of the Son and of the Holy Spirit, teaching them to observe all that I have commanded you" (Matthew 28:19-20).

My question for you is this: If Jesus told the Apostles to teach others what they had been commanded by Him, then doesn't it make sense that whatever the Apostles taught, every preacher and Christian should teach too? Why did man leave out some of the words of the Apostles and especially those of our Lord and Savior Jesus Christ? The answer: Because sometimes man decides for God that His way is no longer the right way. His way was almost two thousand years ago. Man has decided to usurp the authority away from God to himself. What do you think would have happened to the Apostles if they had decided to change the message and command of Jesus? If not then, why today?

For example, Billy Graham says, "He who believes in Jesus will be saved." Why does he leave out the second half of the equation? Jesus said, "Whoever believes and is baptized shall be saved." Saving faith is obedient faith. Mr. Graham takes his passage from Acts 16:30 when the jailor asks Paul and Silas saying, "Sirs, what must I do to be saved?" Paul does say, "Believe in the Lord Jesus, and you will be saved, you and your household." Of course, they are going to have to believe. Paul is not saying just believe, he is telling them that they must believe first.

How do I know this? Because that same night after they "spoke the word of the Lord to him and to all who were in his house…he was baptized at once, he and all his family" (Acts 16:32-33). You see Paul would never leave out baptism. How could he? He was asked why he was waiting so long to be baptized himself. There is no controversy here, just a modern-day problem with following the plain command of Jesus.

I went to one of Mr. Graham's crusades. Oh, how I loved hearing him proclaim the love of Jesus and the power of His name. All who heard were enamored with his message. What's disturbing to me, though, is that it seems he left off part of the message. He told the thousands in attendance that they should come to the front of the stage to receive Christ if they believed. More people than I could count went to the front of the stage. Mr. Graham had them all say a prayer of forgiveness. But there should have been more. Unlike Lydia and the jailor and his family, none of them were baptized at the time they acknowledged Christ. If I had the opportunity to speak with Mr. Graham, I'd ask him, "Why did you not baptize them for the forgiveness of their sins?" What would Paul and Silas say today to those who leave out baptism? Mr. Graham offered only part of the truth.

Mr. Osteen says at the end of every sermon to the folks watching on television, "Say this prayer with me. 'Lord Jesus, I repent of my sins; come into my heart; I make you the Lord of my life.'" Then he says, "If you just did that, we believe that you just got born again." Sometimes he changes it and says, "If you stood up by faith just now, we believe that you were just washed in the blood of Jesus."

Mr. Osteen brings people half-truths. Why does he not say what Peter said on his first sermon, "Repent and be baptized . . . in the name of Jesus Christ for the forgiveness of your sins" (Acts 2:38). Mr. Osteen says to "Repent and ask Him into your heart." Peter says, "Repent and be baptized!" Whom are you going to believe? Mr. Osteen is leading people down a path of destruction. If he is ignorant, then I will pray that his heart will receive the truth. If he knows exactly what he's doing, then I pray that God will give him enough time to repent of the sin of being a false teacher.

I am not Billy Graham or Joel Osteen, and I recognize that God is their final judge. However, I cannot stay silent while these men preach about God and His mercy, love, and grace, only to then see them leave out part of the truth from Jesus Christ Himself on how to be saved. Remember, each of us is going to stand before God. "For we must all appear before the judgment seat of Christ, so that each one may receive what is due for what he has done in the body, whether good or evil. Therefore, knowing the fear of the Lord, we persuade others" (2 Corinthians 5:10-11). Each of us must give an account of whom we have followed. We will be responsible for reading the Word of God for ourselves, and deciding what we will do with it.

Lastly, the Apostle Paul said to saved Christians who were being persecuted: "In flaming fire, inflicting vengeance on those who do not know God and on those who do not obey the gospel of our Lord Jesus. They will suffer the punishment of eternal destruction, away from the presence of the Lord and from the glory of his might" (2 Thessalonians 1:8-9). Did you catch that? "On those who do not know God and on those who do not obey the Gospel." He who believes and is baptized shall be saved.

Is Hell Really Worth It? Three Passages

"For if God did not spare angels when they sinned, but cast them into hell and committed them to chains of gloomy darkness to be kept until the judgment; if he did not spare the ancient world, but preserved Noah, a herald of righteousness, with seven others, when he brought a flood upon the world of the ungodly; if by turning the cities of Sodom and

Gomorrah to ashes he condemned them to extinction, making them an example of what is going to happen to the ungodly; and if he rescued righteous Lot . . . then the Lord knows how to rescue the godly from trials, and to keep the unrighteous under punishment until the day of judgment" (2 Peter 2:4-7, 9).

"Now I want to remind you, although you once fully knew it, that Jesus, who saved a people out of the land of Egypt, afterward destroyed those who did not believe. And the angels who did not stay within their own position of authority, but left their proper dwelling, he has kept in eternal chains under gloomy darkness until the judgment of the great day" (Jude 5-6).

"Sheol [Hell] beneath is stirred up to meet you when you come; it rouses the shades to greet you, all who were leaders of the earth; it raises from their thrones all who were kings of the nations. All of them will answer and say to you: 'You too have become as weak as we! You have become like us!' Your pomp is brought down to Sheol, the sound of your harps; maggots are laid as a bed beneath you, and worms are your covers" (Isaiah 14:9-11).

No one expects to go to hell. Everyone thinks they're going to heaven. Everyone seems to have a myriad of reasons why they believe they will be in heaven over hell. Some say, "I am a good person," while another says, "I feel it in my heart." Still someone else says, "Here is what my pastor told me." My friend, none of those three answers will work for you on Judgment Day. The right answer is that your sins have been taken away, washed in the blood of Jesus. No one is good, "for all have sinned and fall short of the glory of God" (Romans 3:23) and because of this "the wages of sin is death" (Romans 6:23a). That death is right above this paragraph and below your feet.

"But as for the cowardly, the faithless, the detestable, as for murderers, the sexually immoral, sorcerers, idolaters, and all liars, their portion will be in the lake that burns with fire and sulfur, which is the second death" (Revelation 21:8).

I was destined for hell until God changed my life. I pray the same for you. Born once, die twice; born twice, die once. This means after being born physically, each man or woman is destined to die physically and spiritually. However, if you are born a second time, in Christ, you are saved from the spiritual death, saved from hell. You will avoid the second death; you will avoid hell; you will avoid eternal punishment. You will be awarded and rewarded eternal life of peace with Almighty God. "But the free gift of God is eternal life in Christ Jesus our Lord" (Romans 6:23b). Born twice, die once.

Our Lord and Savior Jesus Christ says, "And if your eye causes you to sin, tear it out and throw it away.

It is better for you to enter life with one eye than with two eyes to be thrown into the hell of fire" (Matthew 18:9). I would like to give you the pictures of all pictures that God's Word gives to us when life is over. "Before him will be gathered all the nations, and he will separate people one from another as a shepherd separates the sheep from the goats. And he will place the sheep on his right, but the goats on the left. Then the King will say to those on his right, 'Come, you who are blessed by my Father, inherit the kingdom prepared for you from the foundation of the world'" (Matthew 25:32-34). "Then he will say to those on his left, 'Depart from me, you cursed, into the eternal fire prepared for the devil and his angels'" (Matthew 25: 41).

If you are now ready to avoid all this … if you are scared *to* death, or scared *of* death … if you want God to save you, then you will ask the same question that I asked, the same question 3,000 people asked the first time that the Apostle Peter preached: "What shall we [I] do?" (Acts 2:37).

My friend, the answer never changes. "Repent and be baptized every one of you in the name of Jesus Christ for the forgiveness of your sins, and you will receive the gift of the Holy Spirit" (Acts 2:38). That gift is the saving of your soul.

Please don't gamble with God!

Divisions in the Church! Is Christ Divided?

The Apostle Paul begged one congregation to stop doing something before it got too far down the line to stop. Do you know what that was? Not to divide the church or follow after another man!

Listen closely to what Paul says, "I appeal to you, brothers, by the name of our Lord Jesus Christ, that all of you agree, and that there be no divisions among you, but that you be united in the same mind and the same judgment. For it has been reported to me by Chloe's people that there is quarreling among you, my brothers. What I mean is that each one of you says, 'I follow Paul,' or 'I follow Apollos,' or 'I follow Cephas [Peter],' or 'I follow Christ.' Is Christ divided?" (1 Corinthians 1:10-13a).

Unfortunately for Paul and for the rest of the Apostles and especially for Jesus Christ Himself, the division Paul warned about has happened. Paul names himself, Apollos, and Peter. Well, Peter came first. Jesus established His church in AD 33. The church that would call Peter the first pope was begun around 606 by Boniface. Can you see where I am going with this? Let me rephrase what Paul said using today's twenty-first-century churches. "Now each of you says, 'I am a Catholic,' or 'I am a Baptist,' or 'I am a Lutheran,' or 'I am of Christ.' Is Christ divided?"

Listen to what Paul says next to that church in Corinth. "Was Paul crucified for you? Or were you baptized in the name of Paul?" (1 Corinthians 1:13b). Paul was trying to tell them, as he would today, that there is only one name under heaven by which man will be saved: Jesus Christ. Someone then probably asked Paul, "Can't we break off into groups and follow a certain teacher who still preaches Jesus Christ?" I believe that to be a fair question. However, the problem is and always will be, that every man begins to put a spin or completely change what Jesus Christ has taught. Today, according to man, there are about four or five different ways to be saved. Denominations teach different things about the subject of baptism, tithing, forfeiting salvation, saved by faith alone, and the list goes on and on.

Even more disturbing than that, I share with you something alarming to consider: The Lutheran Church began in the 1500s, Calvinism began in the 1500s, the Baptist Church was founded by John Smyth in the late 1500s, the Methodist Church founded by John Wesley in the 1700s, the Mormon Church was founded in the 1800s by Joseph Smith and the Jehovah's Witnesses by Charles Taze Russell in 1870. Why would any man start a church that was already in place?

Can Jesus Christ our Lord be happy that what began as His church suddenly became another man's idea about his church, and that man called that church some other name?

The very church that Jesus died for has been split, divided, yet it still remains. Are you a part of His church?

I am concerned for you if the church where you attend isn't found in the pages of God's Word. If a Baptist holds up the Word of God and says, "We only preach from the Bible" and a Lutheran says, "We only preach from the Bible," then my question has and will continue to be, "Why do you have different names and different doctrines?" Can you both be right concerning what Jesus teaches when both groups disagree on various topics?

Mind you, I have only used the name of two different church groups. Next, a man says, "I'm Catholic." Now we have total chaos. The Baptist and Lutheran churches don't follow the pope. They have no hierarchy as the Catholics—pope, cardinal, bishop, priest, layman. The other two churches have elders and deacons. Now someone comes along and says, "There's a new revelation that God gave us." Before you know it another group is formed called the Mormon Church. Their church has modern day apostles in addition to elders and deacons.

All the churches that I have mentioned so far all claim to teach only the Bible. But the Mormons have added a new book called *The Book of Mormon*. They go all over the world and convert people to their church. The Baptists convert people into the Baptist Church; others who are looking for God might turn to the Lutheran doctrine. Then there stand the Catholic masses following the pope.

If we took a poll of religious and non-religious people, and asked them who is right, I have a hunch that the answers in both groups would be about the same—that is, they're all right! As long as they believe in Jesus as the Son of God they will all go to heaven. That is a very comforting position to take for sure. I once took that position myself until I started reading the Bible for myself. I wanted to find the truth as to what church I should belong to. I decided to read for myself about the church that Jesus died for and determine whom I would worship with.

As I read, the first group that came to my mind was the Catholic Church. I have many, many friends and family who are Catholic. I learned from the Scriptures that I was going to stand alone on Judgment Day without any of my friends and family to support me. I don't and won't ever have any animosity toward anyone of that faith, but I knew within the first four books of the New Testament that Catholic teaching is very different from what Jesus and the rest of the Apostles taught. Tradition (the Catholics say) is to be held as the highest authority in the church, even above the Bible. George M. Searle wrote in *Plain Facts for Fair Minds* (Forgotten Books, 2015, page 154), "Other spiritual books are preferred."

Yet Jesus told a group of religious people, "So for the sake of your tradition you have made void the word of God. You hypocrites! Well did Isaiah prophesy of you, when he said: 'This people honors me with their lips, but their heart is far from me; in vain do they worship me, teaching as doctrines the commandments of men'" (Matthew 15:6-9). God's commandments and man's traditions don't coincide. In fact, the commandment of God was made into nothing because of their tradition. That quickly concerned me about the Catholic statement I just shared with you, "Tradition is to be held as the highest authority." This proposition goes directly against the will of Jesus.

Next, I found in a book about the Catholic Church that the pope forbade that individuals read the Bible; it's not to be read by all people. The rubber just hit the road for me. Remember earlier I had mentioned that I was told not to read the Bible by the catechism teacher. At the time, I had found that very convenient. But now having read the Bible, not only was I concerned about me, I was concerned about everyone else that I knew who had been told the same thing.

What Jesus said next was what convinced my heart that the church that I was part of from my birth could not be the church that Jesus is talking about. In Matthew 23:9 Jesus said these words, "And call no man your father on earth, for you have one Father, who is in heaven." I had always wondered why I would step into the confessional where the first words out of my mouth were, "Bless me, Father, for I have sinned." Now I had my answer: I wasn't supposed to. This is no indictment on the men who would listen to my confession, but what Jesus commanded in not calling this man father, the Catholic Church endorsed.

When Jesus our Lord was talking to His disciples about the Jewish leaders in Matthew 23, He is trying to get them to see that the leaders love to have their deeds seen and honored by other people. Jesus now tells his disciples "But you [as apostles or Christians] are not to be called rabbi by others." Jesus is teaching a wonderful principle for all time: that "you have one teacher [Jesus, God, Holy Spirit], and you are all brothers" (Matthew 23:8).

Our Lord is doing two things here. First, He is strengthening them to be able to say no to anyone who would ever bow to them or place them as equals to God and his authority; second, He is warning them not to fall into judgment from God and be deemed to be guilty of "teaching as doctrines the commandments of men" (Matthew 15:9).

Jesus continues His teaching: "And call no man your father on earth, for you have one Father, who is in heaven" (Matthew 23:9) First, He commands that they don't let anyone call them by the title "Rabbi," then he tells the crowds and his disciples not to put any man up on such a pedestal as to call him "father," as if he is to be yielded or submitted to. Yes, of course a child is able to call his dad father; indeed, the child is to honor and obey him in this life and under his roof. Jesus is by no means addressing normal life on earth (look at the context) but is teaching them spiritual truths. Not calling any man by an authoritative spiritual name is one of them.

1 love the Lord's final statement "the greatest among you shall be your servant" (Matthew 23:11). Those highest in serving God are the ones who serve without wanting to be noticed or greeted in public a certain way or being referred to by an authoritative public name. God is our Father. We pray, "Our Father in heaven." No man has the power to forgive sins, only our Heavenly Father.

My conscience could no longer allow me to be part of this church. I know that one day I will stand before Jesus Christ and have to give an account of how

I would worship him. The book of Acts, and chapter 11 told me that they were first called Christians in Antioch. From that day forward, I would no longer call myself a Catholic.

Did you know?

- Peter was married. (Matthew 8:14) {This would go against Catholic tradition.}
- Peter refused anyone to bow down to him. (He tolerated no worship to him, unlike the pope today.)
- Peter was never in Rome.

Did you know?

- Mary sinned like the rest of us? She said, "And my spirit rejoices in God my Savior" (Luke 1:47). Mary needed a Savior, too!
- Saying five Hail Marys does not remove your sins! This is not in the Bible!

Mary was blessed to be chosen of God to carry the Savior of the world in her womb. Blessed means "fortunate." It is true that all nations would call her blessed. Mary was blessed but not sinless. She was blessed but not someone to be worshiped or who is a go-between with God. She would be like Paul or Peter or any of the other Apostles who would say, "Get up— do not bow to me!"

Did you know?

The Catholic Church says priests are appointed. But God says in the Bible that all Christians are priests! The Apostle Peter told a group of Christians: "You are a chosen race, a royal priesthood" (1 Peter 2:9).

Did you know?

Priests in the Catholic tradition have to vow a life of celibacy. But God says in the Bible, "To the unmarried and the widows I say that it is good for them to remain single, as I am. But if they cannot exercise self-control, they should marry. For it is better to marry than to burn with passion" (1 Corinthians 7:8-9).

Did you know?

A Catholic is told not to eat meat on Fridays during Lent. But the Bible says: "Now the Spirit expressly says that in later times some will depart from the faith by devoting themselves to deceitful spirits and teachings of demons, through the insincerity of liars whose consciences are seared, who forbid marriage and require abstinence from foods that God created to be received with thanksgiving by those who believe and know the truth." (1 Timothy 4:1-3).

Here are a few more things taught in the Catholic tradition, which are not found in the Bible:

- Purgatory—No mention in the Bible (see Luke 16).

- Confirmation—No commandment for confirmation in the Bible.
- Baby baptism—Not one account in the Bible of babies specifically being baptized, only accounts of the baptisms of those who can believe.
- Cardinals—None found in the Bible.
- The Catholic Church name—Not found in the Bible.

With only concern in my heart, I think I now know why I was told not to read the Bible. I love anyone and all who are Catholic for one reason—truth! I want to share the truth to as many people as I can before I leave this earth and meet Jesus on Judgment Day.

I want everyone I know to have the same fair opportunity to decide for themselves. I want everyone to have a chance to investigate and compare what he or she knows or has been taught with what the Bible teaches. Remember this one thing: The Bible is taught by the Catholic Church, but many Catholics have very little knowledge of what it says because of being told not to read it. Please don't gamble your soul with Almighty God. Read it for yourself.

Jesus said, "I will build my church." The Apostle Paul said that there is "One body." Can you find the name of your church in the Bible? Did you know that the word "church" is said 112 times in the New Testament? Not one time does it say the Catholic, Baptist,

Lutheran, Methodist, Episcopalian, Adventist, or any of the other denominational churches. So, when the Bible says church, do you automatically assume that Jesus is talking about yours? If so, then that would mean all others are excluded.

Was Jesus a Baptist? Lutheran? Catholic? Methodist? I have asked a few random people, "Why do you call yourself a Lutheran?"

I don't know," is the answer that always comes back. Martin Luther himself said, "Do not call yourselves after me." He knew what the Apostle Paul said to the very first church that was attempting to do what eventually the twenty-first century has done—that is, divide the church that belongs to Christ. Did you know that in all the letters to the different churches written to by Paul, there was never a personal name attached to them?

Here is the list of the names of churches that Paul addressed his letters to:
- "to all those in Rome" (Romans 1:7) {to those in Italy}
- "to the church of God that is in Corinth" (1 Corinthians 1:2)
- "to the churches of Galatia" (Galatians 1:2)
- "to the saints who are in Ephesus" (Ephesians 1:1)

- "to all the saints in Christ Jesus who are at Philippi" (Philippians 1:1) {Please note: all Christians are saints, not just when they are dead, like the Catholic Church teaches.}
- "to the saints and faithful brothers in Christ at Colossae" (Colossians 1:2)
- "To the church of the Thessalonians in God the Father and the Lord Jesus Christ" (1 Thessalonians 1:1)
- "The churches of Christ greet you" (Romans 16:16)

The word *church* from the Greek word *ekklesia* means people "called out." By definition, the letters that Paul wrote could easily read like this: *to the "people called out of Galatia" or "to the people called out of God which is at Corinth."*

How does that sound using the denominational names today? To the Baptist people called out, to the Catholic people called out, to the Lutheran people called out.... It sounds exactly how it really is—confusing. People being called out to different groups who teach so differently shows that we have come to the point that there are four or five different ways to be saved.

When I first got saved I wanted to know the difference between denominations. Sadly, I found out that each group had followed the teaching of one man.

Is this what God wants? Did Joseph Smith really want to be the guy that started a church and put a new name to it? Did Martin Luther set out to leave the Catholic Church only then to have everyone who is listening to him call themselves after him? He said no! With the hearts of so many people searching for the truth, is it right that he or she makes the decision based on what the family has always done in the past?

As I was "born a Catholic," did I have a choice in the matter? If my dad was a Lutheran, does that mean I am too? I am sure that there are many more people in the world besides myself who have questioned the very same things I am sharing with you in this book. I mourn for all the people in Rome today who pledge allegiance to whoever is the pope without ever questioning a thing. The pope came about only because of one simple Scripture and conversation between Peter and our Lord Jesus Christ—the same way that God had one small conversation with Adam and Eve. Who has interfered in both cases? You guessed it. The Devil. He tempted Eve just enough to eat something God said not to. In the same way, man has been tempted and deceived just enough to believe that Jesus somehow crowned Peter as the first pope when he said, "I will give you the keys of the kingdom of heaven" (Matthew 16:19).

How did this happen? Well, it's not very difficult. It is all in the desire. The Jews desired so much for
the Messiah to come. They had been told for generations to wait for the Messiah. But these generations
had their minds made up that the Messiah was coming
to set up an earthly kingdom. No one expected that
Jehovah would send the Messiah as one being born to
a virgin in Bethlehem. No one expected Jesus to do all
the miracles he did. And the Jews certainly could never
believe that this Jesus could be the Messiah after he
said that he was the Son of God and that he was going
to destroy the temple. Finally, to a Jew, how could Jesus
be the Messiah if he said, "My kingdom is not of this
world" (John 18:36).

An entire nation's desire was locked into what
they wanted instead of seeing what God wanted. In
the same way, men and women today, with an earnest
desire to please God, have fallen into the same trap.
No, the Catholic Church isn't looking for an earthly
kingdom, but instead has set up an earthly king (the
pope) between man and God thinking that this is what
God wants. It sounds good. "You are Peter, and on this
rock I will build my church, and the gates of hell shall
not prevail against it. I will give you the keys of the
kingdom of heaven, and whatever you bind on earth
shall be bound in heaven" (Matthew 16:18-19).

"You are Peter." *Petros* means *a stone*. Peter as a stone should be firm, immovable, and fixed on his preaching. No doubt Peter and his energy and boldness served to mold and grow the church that began in Jerusalem. Peter, James, and John were almost inseparable in their teaching on the streets to anyone who would listen.

"Upon this rock." This word *petra* refers to the foundation upon which Jesus built his church. *Petros*, which means *a stone* would certainly refer to Peter. Jesus said upon this rock—*petra*, meaning the truth that Peter had just confessed. He confessed that Jesus Christ is the Son of the living God!

"I will build my church." This is in the future. Jesus will. He had not yet. His church will begin in Jerusalem on the day of Pentecost (a Jewish celebration, where all nations would be there). His church is derived from the Greek *ekklesia*, which means *called out* or *assembly*. Here, "my church" means the assembly or people who have been called out of the world by the Gospel of Christ.

"And the gates of hell shall not prevail against it" means the powers of hell. Jesus began building his people one by one, day by day, and no one can stop the power of the message that contains the forgiveness of sins.

"I will give you the keys of the kingdom of heaven" simply means, "I will give you (and the other Apostles too) the terms and conditions of admitting people into the church." *The keys* is a figure of speech, as it is in this passage: "the words of the holy one, the true one, who has the key of David" (Revelation 3:7). Listen to similar language spoken in the Old Testament by the prophet Isaiah: "And I will place on his shoulder the key of the house of David. He shall open, and none shall shut; and he shall shut, and none shall open. And I will fasten him like a peg in a secure place, and he will become a throne of honor to his father's house" (Isaiah 22:22-23).

Key, peg, and *throne* are used as figures of speech to describe power and foundation. There are two ways to read and understand what Jesus was trying to convey to Peter and the rest of the Apostles that day.

Which one sounds like what Jesus was saying?

"I will build my church and make you (Peter) to be king and first pope over all people. And when you die, make sure we have an election to make someone else become the next pope, making sure you give him your keys to the kingdom." Did they actually have keys made up for the throne? (You now have what I see as the Catholic Church's interpretation.)

Or, consider this:

"I will build my people, and upon your confession that I am the Son of the living God, I give you the terms and conditions of admitting people into the church. The powers of hell cannot stop it." (You now have the church that Jesus built.)

If Peter was the first pope, one would think that others would have started to call him by that name. Secondly, I would have at least expected to read about people bowing and falling to their knees in great respect. I read just the opposite: "When Peter entered, Cornelius met him and fell down at his feet and worshiped him. But Peter lifted him up, saying, 'Stand up; I too am a man'" (Acts 10:25-26). Peter, and for that matter, all the Apostles who had the keys to admittance into Jesus' church, would say the same thing. "Stand up, I too am a man."

Paul and Barnabas did. "Men, why are you doing these things? We also are men, of like nature with you" (Acts 14:15). Lastly, the Apostle John wrote for all of us to read and understand this continual concept. An angel said to John, "These are the true words of God" (Revelation 19:9) Here is how John reacted. "Then I fell down at his feet to worship him, but he said to me, 'You must not do that! I am a fellow servant with you and your brothers who hold to the testimony of Jesus. Worship God!'" (Revelation 19:10).

I know that we all want to believe anyone who is sincere in telling us spiritual truths. It makes some sense why people would flock to and bow down and worship the pope thinking that this is what God had intended. I believe that people are inherently sincerely trying to do good, do right, and follow God in the process. But I also know that sincerity of heart is not enough to save a man. The Bible says that Cornelius was "a devout man who feared God with all his household, gave alms generously to the people, and prayed continually to God" (Acts 10:2). An angel of the Lord went to Cornelius's house to tell him that God had heard his prayers and that his alms had ascended as a memorial to God. However, he would need to hear the words that the Apostle Peter was going to tell him in order to be saved.

Peter spoke the Word of God to him right after Cornelius said this: "Now therefore we are all here in the presence of God to hear all that you have been commanded by the Lord" (Acts 10:33). Wow! What a soft, humble heart. He could have said, "I know that an angel has told me to listen to you, but I'm a good person and I've been taught by my parents what to believe." He simply said to Peter what the angel said to him with all humility. "Ask for Simon who is called Peter. He is lodging in the house of Simon, a tanner, by the sea. So

I sent for you at once, and you have been kind enough to come" (Acts 10:32-33a).

I am hoping that if you are Catholic and reading this right now, that you might have the same disposition of heart that Cornelius had. I am not an Apostle or an angel. I am simply trying to be like the Apostle Peter in distributing the keys to the kingdom of heaven. I want to give you the keys so that you might use them to open the door to heaven for your soul. I am not trying to hurt or insult you. I just want to follow the Lord's command: "Go therefore and make disciples of all nations, baptizing them in the name of the Father and of the Son and of the Holy Spirit" (Matthew 28:19). I care about your soul so much that I am willing to risk the possibility that you will never want to speak with me again. I would rather gamble on God and take the risk in hopes of you becoming a Christian, than to have you look at me on Judgment Day and ask me why I never told you.

I know that there is a very good chance you were baptized as a baby and later confirmed in the Catholic Church. My friend or family member, you won't be able to find that in the Word of God. I have looked for twenty-plus years. Please search the Scriptures for yourself. I know that God would want you to. He "is patient toward you, not wishing that any should perish, but that all should reach repentance" (2 Peter 3:9). May God grant you enough days.

There are so many reasons I couldn't be a Catholic, Baptist, Lutheran, or a new group called Mormon. They claim new revelation in the 1800s. First, the pope claims to receive revelation by *ex-cathedra* or when sitting in a special chair; next a man named Joseph Smith claims that the Angel Moroni visited him with new revelation. The Bible says, "For God is not a God of confusion but of peace" (1 Corinthians 14:33). Yet many in the world say, "Join the church of your choice." One group claims God speaks to them; another group says that God sent an angel to tell them something else. In my pursuit for the truth, it was very easy to eliminate the Mormon Church because of what I just said and what the Apostle Paul said to the Galatians. "But even if we or an angel from heaven should preach to you a gospel contrary to the one we preached to you, let him be accursed" (Galatians 1:8).

Did you know that the people of Islam claim that their prophet Mohammed was visited by the Angel Gabriel? Do you see what's going on here? Would our loving God who gave us Jesus, give us conflicting and confusing information long after the Word of God was put together for our instruction? Does God send the Angel Gabriel to one group and give them one set of instructions only to turn right around and give a whole new set of instructions to another group? Of course not. These new divisions came hundreds (thousands!) of years too late for me to follow.

I know these statements may be hard to hear, and even harder to digest and take to heart. I exhort you, my friends, to read the Bible for yourself. Measure your personal faith and traditions against Scripture, and see what God reveals to you.

From the days of the Apostles, there was one church of Jesus Christ, with a single body of doctrine taught by the Apostles. They preached repentance, confession, and baptism. When people heard the message of Jesus on the cross they believed in Him as Savior, the forgiver of sins, and Jesus as the Son of God. The Apostles would tell them to repent, confess, and be baptized for the remission of their sins, making them Christians and children of God.

I sincerely ask you to look at this chart and ask yourself one question: If Jesus established His church in A.D. 33, why would it be necessary to start a new one? Call it some other name? And have it founded by someone other than Jesus Christ? Aren't we called Christians? After the Christ? Is this not a picture of Christ divided?

CHURCH	PLACE	DATE	FOUNDER
Roman Catholic	Rome, Italy	606	Boniface III
Lutheran	Augsburg, Germany	1530	Martin Luther
Presbyterian	Switzerland	1535	John Calvin
Baptist	London, England	1607	John Smyth
Methodist	London, England	1729	John Wesley
Mormon	New York	1830	Joseph Smith
Jehovah's Witnesses	Pennsylvania	1874	Charles T. Russell
Jesus Christ "I will build my church."	**Jerusalem**	**33**	**Jesus Christ**

Chapter ⚃⚃

Will You Gamble Your Soul on Judgment Day?

Are you confident on the Judgment Day that you can look Jesus in the eye and tell him that you were a Baptist, Mormon, or Catholic? Can you look Him in the eye and say, "I was named a Lutheran?" Please remember this Scripture from the Apostle Peter: "And there is salvation in no one else, for there is no other name under heaven given among men by which we must be saved" (Acts 4:12).

Will the pope be there next to you on Judgment Day to plead your case to Christ? No, it will be you alone before the judgment seat of Christ (2 Corinthians 5:10). There will be no party or family of four going to the judgment together. There will be no excuses like, "Well, that's what my parents told me" or "My spouse was this, so I followed him." No one will be able to submit their 5,000 Hail Marys because Mary herself would tell you not to hail her in the first place. The moment we die, we will know where our eternity will be.

While it is today, will you consider obeying the Gospel call right now? The choice is yours. Before you decide to say no, listen to the Apostle Paul. The Lord Jesus will be "revealed from heaven with his mighty angels in flaming fire, inflicting vengeance on those who do not know God and on those who do not obey the gospel of our Lord Jesus" (2 Thessalonians 1:7-8).

You may be curious about the church I decided to follow, what its name is.

"Christians Meet Here" is the name of our church. It is a "Church of Christ," like the one referenced in Romans 16:16. Can't we all just be Christians?

"Whoever believes and is baptized will be saved" (Mark 16:16).

During my journey toward the truth about Jesus Christ, God answered my cry to Him by providentially putting three people in my path to plant the Word of God into my heart.

Duncan – I'm Born Again!

Charles – Jesus Christ judges!

Michael – Are you saved?

Are **you** a Born Again Believer in the Savior and Judge Jesus Christ? Are **you** saved?

He Gambled with God No More—He Obeyed the Gospel

It was soon after my mother's death that I knew that I needed to talk to my dad about his mortality. I called him and began to tell him Whom he needed to know and what he must do in order to go to heaven. He could tell by my voice how serious I was. From that point on we began to have weekly Bible studies. I was shocked from the beginning because he had so many questions.

Mind you, some questions usually arise when I have Bible studies, but this was different. He seemed to ask his questions from the perspective of a novice but also as someone who wanted desperately to find the truth despite what he had been told as a boy. He asked many questions about the Apostle Peter and his role in the church and about the preacher, Joel Osteen, whom he had watched on television a few times.

My response to him and to you who are reading this book is always the same. God is always right in spite of what man says. "Dad, I will tell you only what the Word of God (the Bible) says. If I can't find it in the Bible, then I won't say it. But, if I do find it in the Bible, they are God's words and not mine." He agreed and we began to have great discussions about the truth we found in the Scriptures.

We covered many subjects. He asked about being baptized as a baby. I told him that it was wonderful that his parents did that for him, but that it is not found in the Bible. Just as it was not Biblical when he and my mother had baptized me when I was born because of how they had been taught. I brought him to all the Scriptures in the entire Bible so he could see for himself. He was almost in disbelief when I read aloud to him this, "But when they believed Philip as he preached good news about the kingdom of God and the name of Jesus Christ, they were baptized, both men and women" (Acts 8:12). I too remember being astonished when I read that men and women were baptized, not babies.

I began to try to lay out all the dots on baptism hoping that he would connect them. The first dot was when Jesus Himself said, "Whoever believes and is baptized will be saved" (Mark 16:16). Without a word, I could tell that he instantly believed that a person must believe first that Jesus Christ is the Son of God and the Savior of every soul. Jesus said, "I am the way, and the truth, and the life. No one comes to the Father except through me" (John 14:6). He must then be baptized for the forgiveness of his sins, not as a baby but as someone with the ability to understand and respond. I told him, "So faith comes from hearing, and hearing through the word of Christ" (Romans 10:17).

He now knew the truth about the doctrine of babies being baptized was something that man must have come up with. I showed him constantly, again and again, a passage that all men need to hear and come to grips with: "And he said to them, 'Well did Isaiah prophesy of you hypocrites, as it is written, "This people honors me with their lips, but their heart is far from me; in vain do they worship me, teaching as doctrines the commandments of men." You leave the commandment of God and hold to the tradition of men'" (Mark 7:6-8).

Most people have heard of the Ten Commandments that God gave to the children of Israel through Moses. However, most people have never read for themselves what Jesus Christ said to the religious people of His day that applies to all religious people today. People have come up with their own commandments that are not and have never been given by God. I told my dad that as a Christian and now preacher of God's Word, that I cannot give him my opinion. I told him that God not only provides the love and grace but also the message and conditions of pardon. "I can't save you, Dad, but God can."

The Apostle Paul told the young preacher Timothy, "All Scripture is breathed out by God and profitable for teaching, for reproof, for correction, and for training in righteousness" (2 Timothy 3:16).

What that means in terms we can understand is this: God wrote the Bible, and it is valuable for teaching (doctrine), for warning (reproof), for correcting our sins, and teaching us righteous living, so that we Christians will be prepared to live for God.

"Dad," I said, "God tells every man, 'He became the source of eternal salvation to all who obey him' (Hebrews 5:9). Jesus says, 'Unless one is born of water and the Spirit, he cannot enter the kingdom of God' (John 3:5)."

Dad asked me about the Catholic Church. I simply said that I am not a part of the Catholic Church. I told him what Jesus told the Apostle Peter. "I will build my church, and the gates of hell shall not prevail against it" (Matthew 16:18). After reading the Bible for the last nineteen years I found more than enough Scriptures that tell me that this church is filled with the doctrines and commandments of men.

I said, "Dad, I don't want Jesus telling me that my worship was in vain, only then to have him say to me, 'I never knew you; depart from me' (Matthew 7:23). Dad, I have to take the risk of you being angry with me. I don't want you to be asking me on Judgment Day, 'Why didn't you tell me?'"

For all of you who are reading this and are angry or defensive, I only ask you, I beg you, to read all the passages that I have shown you in this book and then decide for yourselves. Please remember this one thing: If you and I both believe that Jesus is the Son of God and the Savior of the world, if we agree that Jesus is the Lamb of God that takes away the sins of the world, and if we agree that whatever Jesus says to do to be saved is what we will do, then wouldn't you agree that there cannot be more than one way to be saved? Therefore, if Jesus Himself says, "Whoever believes and is baptized will be saved," can we not agree that this is what we need to do?

On July 16, 2014, I baptized my dad in the name of Jesus Christ for the remission of his sins. What I want the world to know is what he said just before I baptized him. "I know that if I died today that I would go to hell."

After baptizing him, I told him that all his horrible sins, the sins committed during his marriage, the sins as a man in his twenties, the sins as a teenager were completely wiped clean by the blood of his new Lord and Savior. Now he knew for sure he would spend eternity in heaven.

These days I shed more tears than you can imagine—first for my dad in obeying the Gospel before it was too late and then for all the people I know who may not know the Lord yet. Time is ticking, and the parking meter is running out of the quarters of time that God has put in your earthly life.

One day soon, there won't be another breath that comes from your lungs and out of your mouth; you will be pronounced dead. In the next moment of time, you will know for certain where your next spiritual breath will be taken for all time. A man will hear only one of two phrases when he leaves this world for the next one: "Come, you who are blessed by my Father, inherit the kingdom prepared for you from the foundation of the world" (Matthew 25:34) or "I never knew you; depart from me" (Matthew 7:23).

Do you know Him? I don't mean *about* Him. I mean know Him enough to follow Him? To be born again? To obey the Gospel? If so, then you are described by Jesus Himself in this way: "Everyone then who hears these words of mine and does them will be like a wise man who built his house on the rock" (Matthew 7:24).

As Ananias asked the Apostle Paul, "Why do you wait? Rise and be baptized and wash away your sins, calling on his name" (Acts 22:16).

If you do, you are no longer gambling with God.

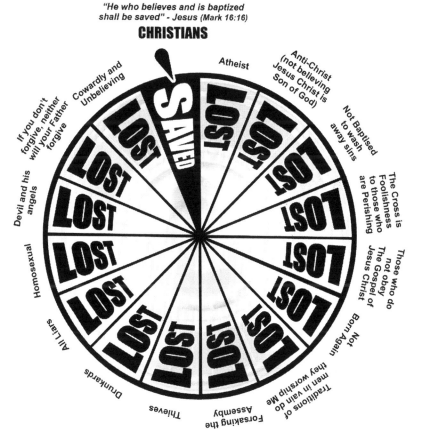

"For the gate is narrow and the way is hard that
leads to life, and those who find it are few."
Matthew 7:14

Medical Evaluation of Your Soul

1. Please check any or all appropriate items listed below that you have done or thought about at least one time:
- ☐ Lied
- ☐ Stolen
- ☐ Cheated
- ☐ Been drunk
- ☐ Hate
- ☐ Pornography
- ☐ Jealous
- ☐ Bitter
- ☐ Fornication
- ☐ Lust
- ☐ Homosexual
- ☐ Adultery

2. If you have checked even one of these, then your CT scan (Christ Test) shows the following:
- We are sorry to tell you that you are TERMI-NALLY ill.
- You have a DISEASE of the SOUL.
- Your body is engulfed and overwhelmed with sin.

TREATMENT

GREAT NEWS! We have caught it in time!! There is a 100% cure to your disease. IT IS THE ONLY

CURE! A great physician named JESUS CHRIST can cure you fully and lead you to a long and active life in service to HIM and your family.

The treatment to remove the DISEASE will take two seconds. Simply believe in this doctor, come to HIM, and be baptized into HIS name!

In two seconds, HE will remove your sins with HIS blood and bring you up out of the water a perfectly healed man! No more DISEASE of your soul, no more SIN, no more walking around day to day with the thought that you are terminally ill. YOU WILL BE SAVED.

QUESTIONS that typical patients have:

1. Is there any other treatment for my disease? NO!
2. Should I get a second opinion before I do this? YES! Please turn to Acts 2:38, Mark 16:16, and Matthew 28:18-20.
3. Can I or should I wait to have this operation? IF you die before having the operation, you will be LOST and the PHYSICIAN cannot help you . . . EVER!
4. If I decide NOT to have the operation, what will happen to me?
   - You will live with vile people who committed the worst atrocities in history, as well as good people like moms, dads, grandmothers and grandfathers, high school students, CEOs, doctors, nurses, teachers, accountants, athletes, entertainers, and

even religious hypocrites who NEVER accepted the CURE!

- YOU will CRY all day long.
- YOU will be in DARKNESS all day long.
- YOU will be in despair and agonizing regret for refusing treatment.
- YOU and anyone who refuses treatment for their sins will be the only ones who will get a FIRSTHAND look at what the DEVIL really looks like.

What could be worse than that?

1. Jesus Christ saying to you, "I never knew you, depart from me into everlasting punishment."
2. MISSING HEAVEN!
3. NOT getting to spend all eternity with AL-MIGHTY GOD who sent the PHYSICIAN just to cure YOU!
4. AND FINALLY . . . You will NEVER be able to spend one more minute with your family and friends who obeyed the Gospel.

Possible Reactions or Side Effects

- Anger and resentment to the one who gave you this bad news.
- Sadness, hurt, shock, and temptation to think "I don't have a disease of the soul." Therefore, you REJECT the treatment.

- No reaction at all. This would be the WORST possible news. Patients with no response have been shown to have no remorse for how they lived (with sin) and no thoughts of GOD in their heart (found after autopsy). OR . . .
- YOU will be moved to receive this treatment and LIVE!
- YOU will be forgiven of ALL your sins!
- YOU will BE SAVED!

Need a Spiritual Physician? Be cured!

About the Author

Tom Covino grew up on the north shore of Long Island; as a child, he experienced the very difficult divorce of his parents that led him down a path of gambling. He spent his young adulthood as a New York gambling bartender until he became a Born Again Christian and Gospel preacher. He is husband to Jennifer and father to two girls, Gwendolyn and Aubrey. Tom has also been a teacher of golf for twenty-plus years and sees a direct correlation between the game of golf and life as a Christian. The most important thing to Tom is the salvation of every soul that he meets.

Made in the USA
Columbia, SC
08 December 2024